FRANCIS FORD COPPOLA

STERLING HAYDEN

DUSTIN HOFFMAN

COEN BROTHERS

ALFRED HITCHCOCK

ORSON ...LLES

BARBARA STANWYCK

JAMES STEWART

H...

...OEL McCREA

FRANÇOIS TRUFFAUT

WOODY ALLEN

BOGART

MARILYN MONROE

ROBERT DE NIRO

FAYE DUNAWAY

MICHAEL CURTIZ

WES ANDERSON

CARY GRANT

ROYAL
NAME THAT
MOVIE

QUEL est ce FILM ?

100 rébus illustrés pour cinéphiles

par PAUL ROGERS

c
am
bou
rakis

TITRE ORIGINAL :
NAME THAT MOVIE

FIRST PUBLISHED IN ENGLISH BY CHRONICLE BOOKS LLC. SAN FRANCISCO, CALIFORNIA.

POUR TOUS CES GENS MERVEILLEUX
ASSIS DANS LE NOIR.

INTRODUCTION

En regardant *Chinatown* pour la quinzième fois peut-être – cette scène en particulier où l'on voit Jake Gittes placer deux montres sous un pneu de la voiture d'Hollis Mulwray –, il m'est venu à l'esprit que si je dessinais ces montres et ce pneu, les gens qui avaient aimé le film se souviendraient comme moi de ce bref passage. De là est née l'idée d'une série de dessins inspirés de grands classiques, qui pourrait offrir un jeu d'énigmes visuelles digne d'intérêt. C'est ainsi que je me suis mis à revisionner un certain nombre de mes films favoris, équipé d'un carnet de croquis, le doigt sur la touche pause de ma télécommande.

J'ai voulu éviter, autant que possible, de dessiner les stars, m'efforçant d'éluder les scènes les plus marquantes pour me concentrer sur des détails originaux. En tant que designer appréciant particulièrement l'architecture et la typographie, je me suis attaché à étudier de près bâtiments et signalétique. Bien que le lettrage – petit ou grand – m'ait toujours sauté aux yeux, je n'avais pas remarqué jusqu'alors l'importance que peuvent prendre les notes manuscrites et autres éléments imprimés dans le déroulement d'une intrigue.

J'ai jugé que six dessins, en séquence, donneraient une bonne idée du film. L'objectif était d'offrir des indices qui provoquent l'étincelle de la mémoire, le souvenir d'un film plutôt que son histoire. Bien sûr, certains offrent des douzaines de plans exploitables, c'était donc un challenge de n'en sélectionner que six. D'autres fois, l'examen s'est révélé beaucoup plus délicat.

J'aime tous les films présents dans ce livre, et si quelques-uns sont connus de tous ou presque, d'autres n'auront pas forcément retenu l'attention du public ; cependant, ce sont tous de grands films. Vous trouverez du Hitchcock (un soupçon), du Billy Wilder, une poignée de vieux films noirs, des blockbusters, quelques films étrangers et finalement un paquet de films 70's. Dans ce contexte ludique et en raison de leur caractère plutôt obscur, j'ai dû mettre de côté certains de mes films préférés (difficile de retrouver le titre d'un film ni vu ni connu). Je suggérerais tout de même que si vous n'avez vu ni *Le Port de la drogue* (1953) ni *Ascenseur pour l'échafaud* (1958) il serait grand temps !

Le livre compte 100 films. Les réponses sont données en fin d'ouvrage. Vous trouverez une liste de titres par ordre d'apparition ainsi qu'un index alphabétique destiné aux lecteurs qui craignent de tomber par inadvertance sur l'une ou l'autre des solutions suivantes. J'espère que vous vous prendrez au jeu, et vous surprendrez à donner de la valeur aux petits détails qui font les grands films.

J'aimerais faire part de ma reconnaissance à l'égard de ma femme Jill, qui a toléré de me voir passer tant de dimanches assis dans le canapé devant la télévision, avec mon carnet de croquis et ma télécommande. Puisque le livre est maintenant terminé, nous allons de nouveau pouvoir sortir le dimanche, aller voir un film peut-être.

Paul Rogers

QUEL *est ce* FILM ?

1

PARIS
9

BLUE PARROT

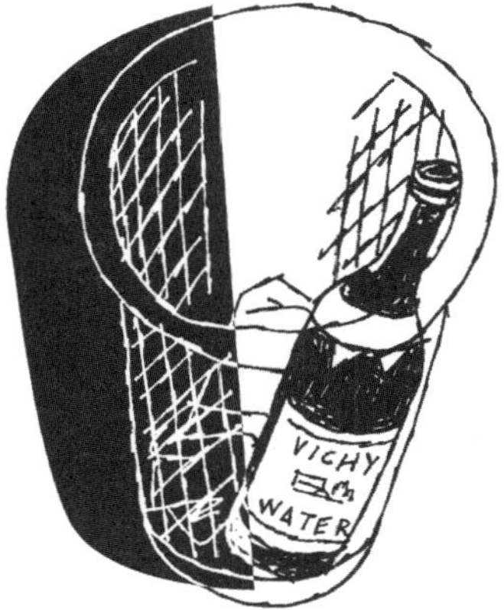
VICHY
WATER

2

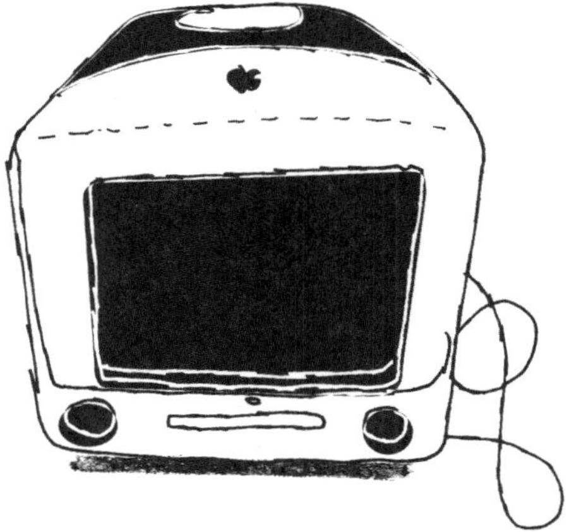

3

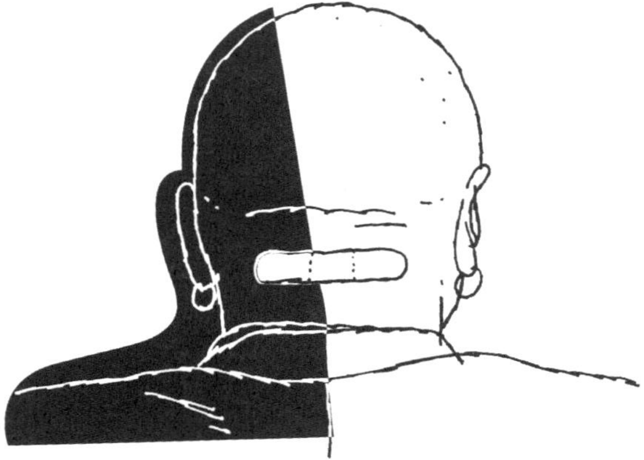

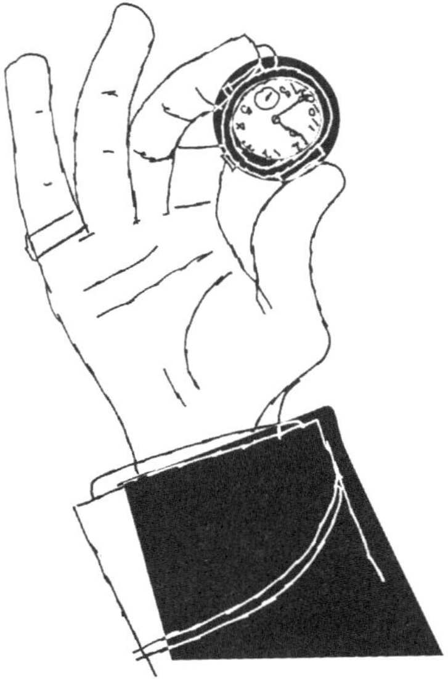

DRIVE IN
RIVER GLEN MOTEL
MOTEL
VACANCY

20933
MONEY TO LOAN
Buy
Sell
Trade
INSTANT CASH
JEWELRY · GOLD · DIAMONDS ·
TV · VCR · TOOLS · WATCHES ·
STEREO · CAMERA
LOAN

Hawthorne
GRILL

4

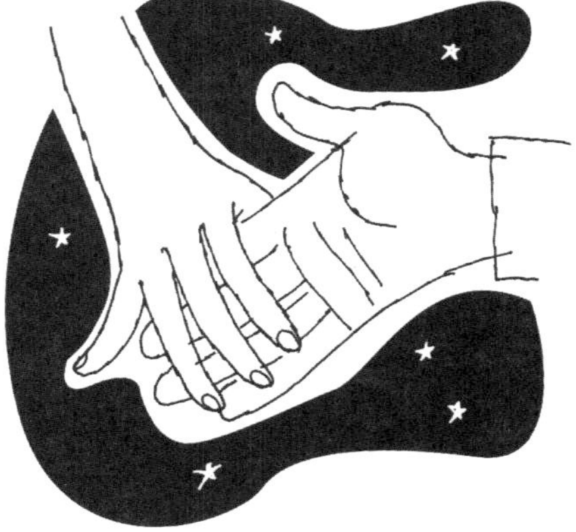

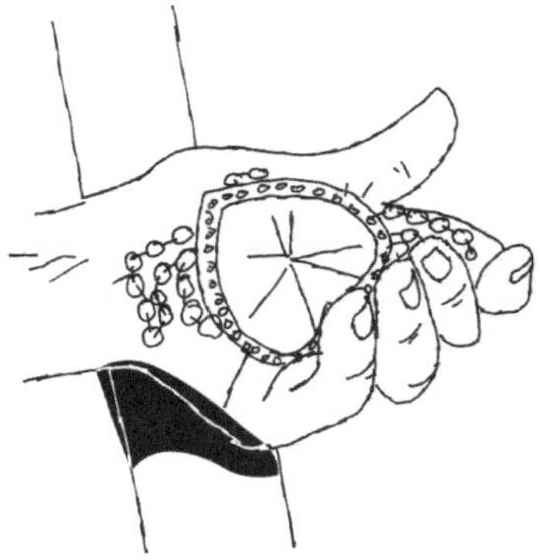

5

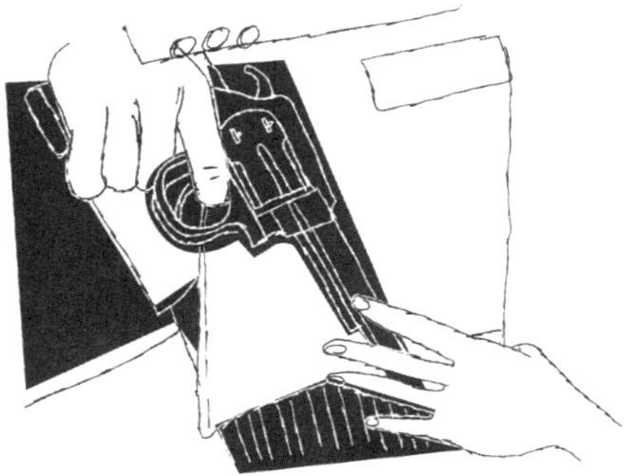

BATON ROUGE, LOUISIANA
WHERE IS HE?
NO TRACE SINCE HE FLED DYING BROTHER
U.S. Delegates Attend Meet

LOVE

6

WOLTZ INTERNATIONAL PICTURES

New York World-Telegram
FINAL
POLICE HUNT COP KILLER
FEDERAL BILL PASSES

PAY
STOP
FARE

El Rancho Vegas
Presents
JOE E. LEWIS
GLORIA De HAVEN
DINING DANCING
GAMING
DANCING
TO THE RITZ
ORCHESTRA
MIDNITE TO 6AM
THE RENEE MOLNAR DANCERS

7

STRIPPERS
The Best Little CHAPEL
The Best Little CHAPEL

FT
2 T

8

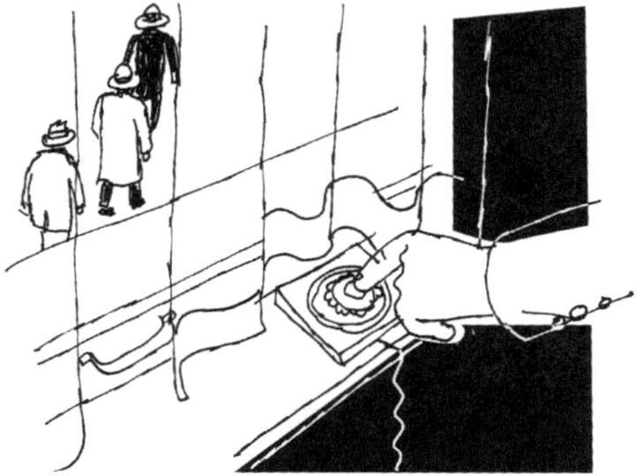

9

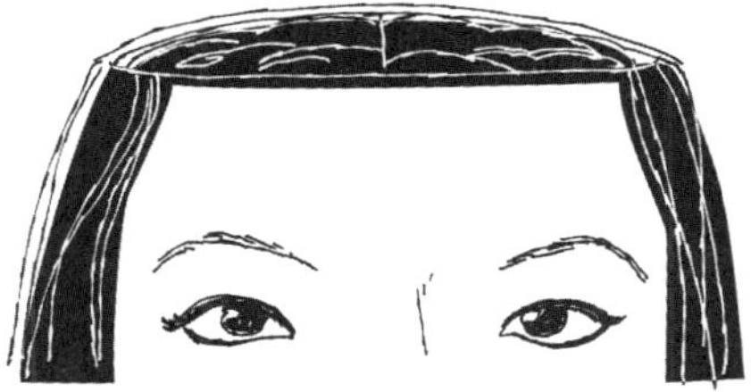

DEATH LIST FIVE
1 OREN ISHII
COTTONMOUTH
2 VERNITA GREEN
COPPERHEAD
3 BUDD
SIDE WINDER
4
5

10

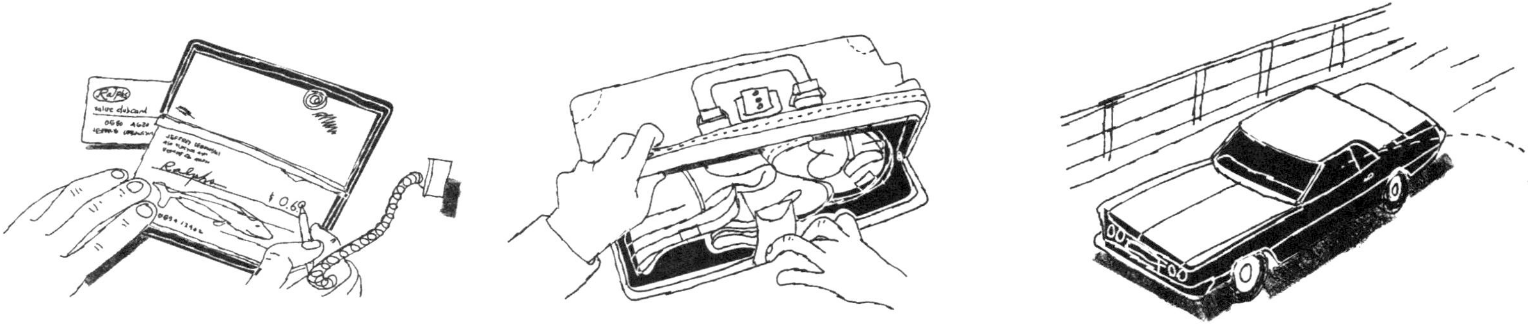

LOGJAMIN'

AUTOBAHN
nagelbett

gers
Roasted

11

SAN FRANCISCO
1. PICKUP MESSAGE
MARK HOPK
HOTEL
2. PHONE CHAL
DO. 4-6823

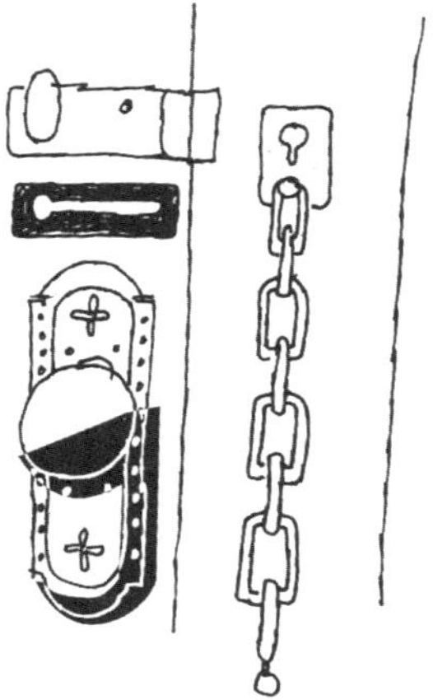

JJZ109

PANAM

12

13

SHOW&TELL
Show&Tell
FRENCH
737

VOTE FOR PALANTINE
PALANTINE FOR PRESIDENT
DONT WALK

LYRIC
2 EXICTING HITS!
BOLD XXX ENTERTAINMENT
"SOMETIME SWEET SUSAN"
ALSO EXPLICT! PROVOCATIVE!
'SWEDISH MARRIGE MANUAL'
TWO BIG HITS
Sometime Sweet Susan

Belmore Cafeteria

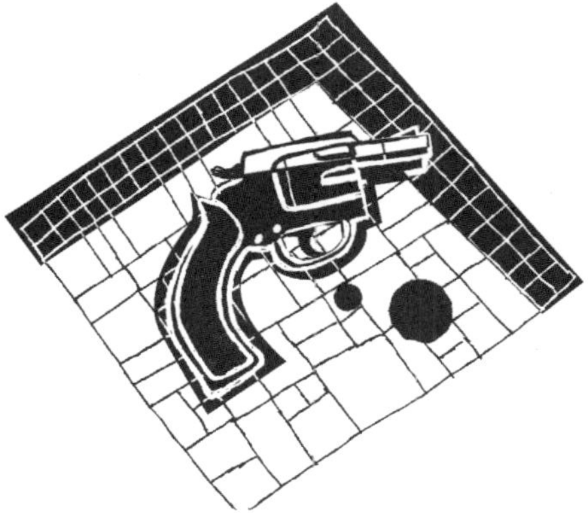

14

ROYAL
SPENCER TRACY
FATHER OF THE BRIDE

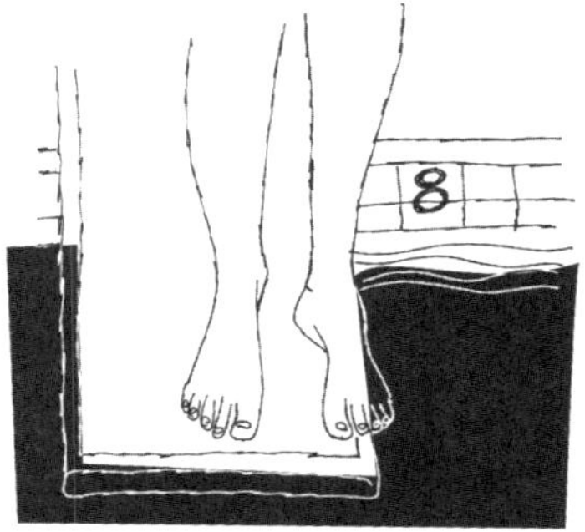
8

SENIOR PICNIC OR BUST
ANARENE HIGH 1952

CACTUS
MOTEL
COMMERCIAL RATES
OFFICE

79
29
TEX CO
TEXAS MOON CAFE

15

FRANK ROSS
BORN
DIED

16

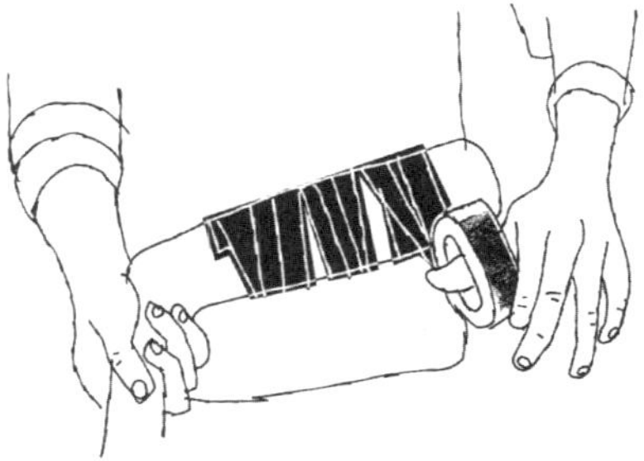

LEONARDO
382
VOLUNTEER
FIRST AID & RESCUE

MILD
SALSA
THICK & CHUNKY

17

LUNCH
GAS
TWIN OAKS
GASOLINE
CIRCLE STAR
MAN WANTED
CHICKEN DINNER
$1.25
BEST IN THE WORLD

Nick -
I'm going away
with Frank -
I love him
Cora

TWIN OAKS
LUNCH BREAKFAST DINNER

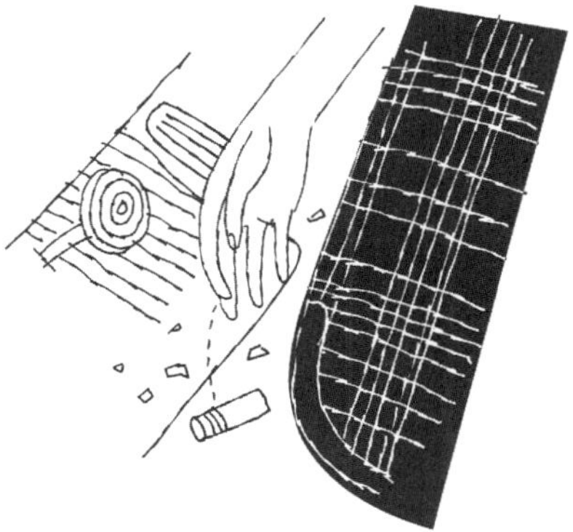

GRAND JURY INDICTS CHAMBERS AS SLAYER

Killed Wife In Bogus Auto Accident, Charge To Face Murder Trial

Sensational Cora Smith Case Has Aftermath in Action Against Husband

18

The Evening Star
Night Final
SPORTS
DIPLOMAT SLAIN AT U.N.
Nixon Promises West Will Remain in Berlin
Assassin Eludes Police Efforts
BULLETIN
RACING RESULTS
Public Hous

R·O·T
R·O·T

ROUTE
41
BUS
STOP

Ambassador Hotels
CHICAGO
SUPERIOR 7200
212 N. Michigan

19

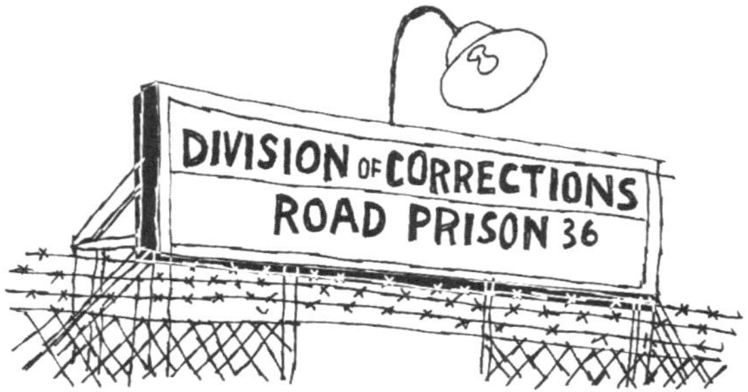
DIVISION OF CORRECTIONS
ROAD PRISON 36

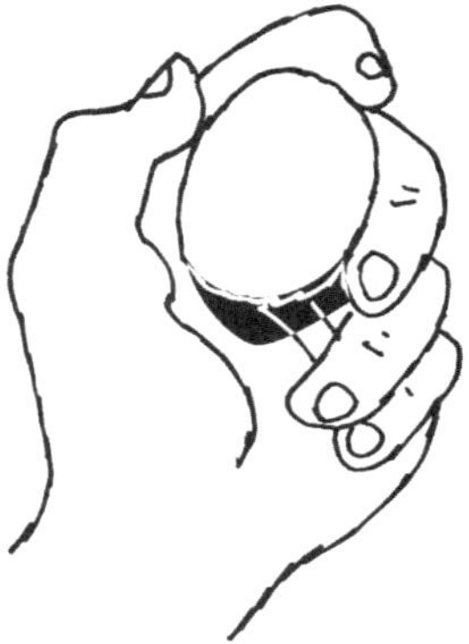

21

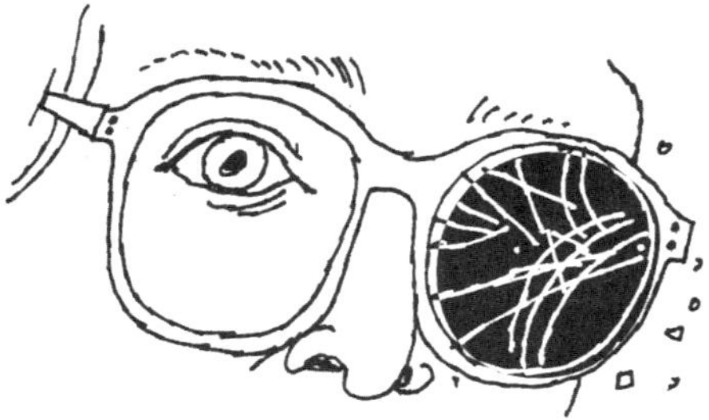

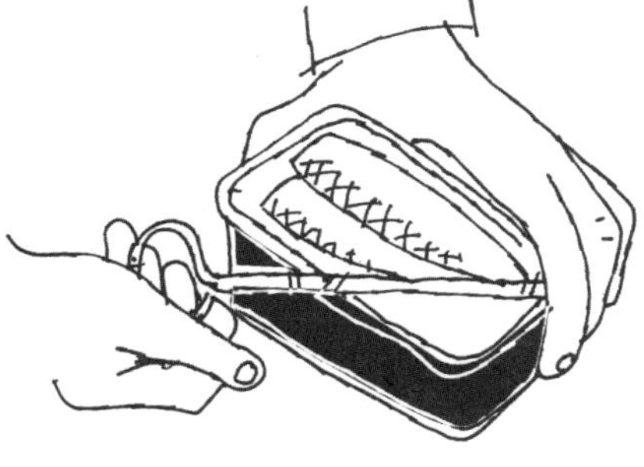

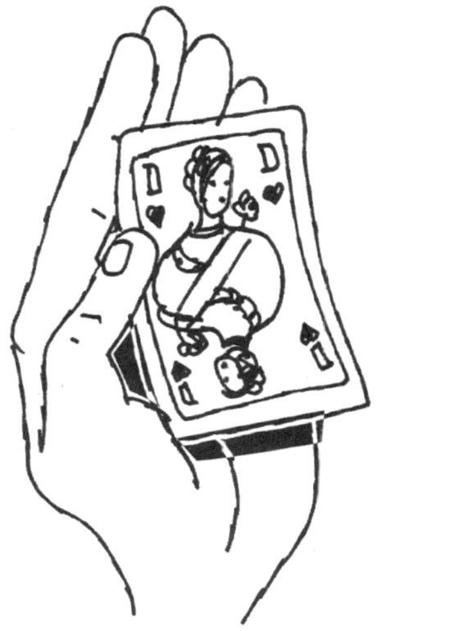

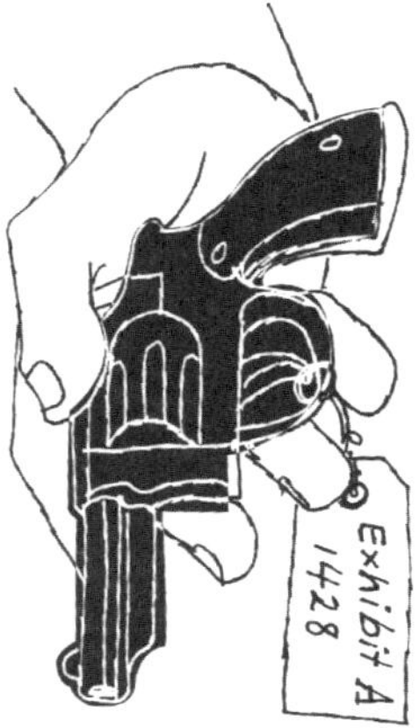
Exhibit A
1428

REAL ESTATE
SEE
WALLY FAY
FOR BEST BUYS IN
REAL ESTATE
WALLY FAY
LOTS • HOUSES
RENTALS
INSURANCE

MILDREDS
HOTEL CLARIDGE
HOTEL
MILDRED'S
M
FI

Society and Clubs
Ladies Guild to Give Buffet Luncheon
Business Woman, Beragon Heir Wed

23

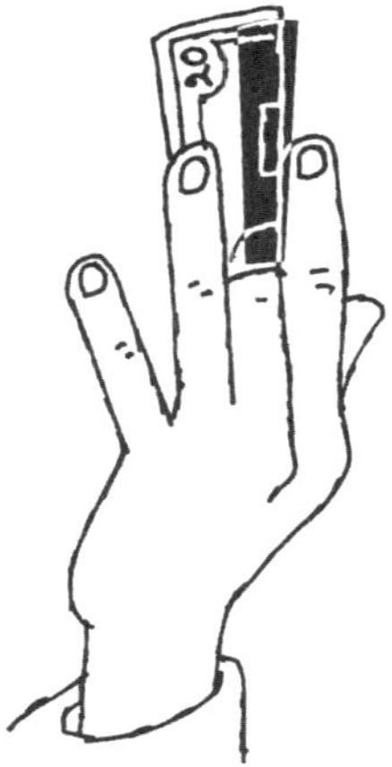

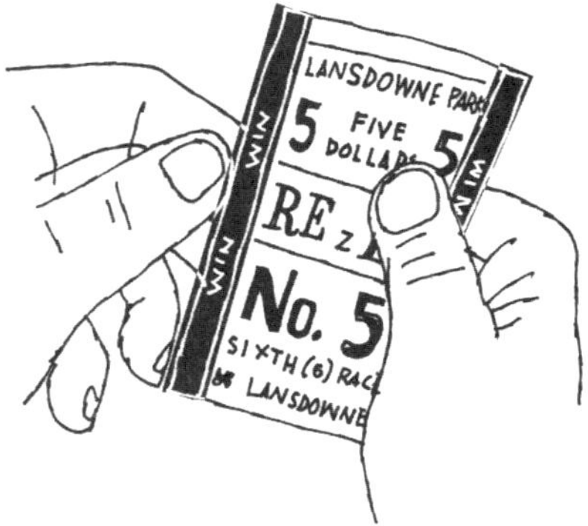
LANSDOWNE PARK
5 FIVE DOLLARS 5
WIN
No. 5
SIXTH (6) RAC
LANSDOWNE

15¢ CHESS 15¢
AND
CHECKERS
PER HOUR

831
MONEY TO LOAN
MA. 8431
WE BUY SELL & TRADE
MONEY TO LOAN ON EVERYTHING
MONEY TO LOAN
MONEY TO LOAN
USE OUR LAY AWAY PLAN
CLEARANCE
MONEY TO BUY
MONEY TO BUY

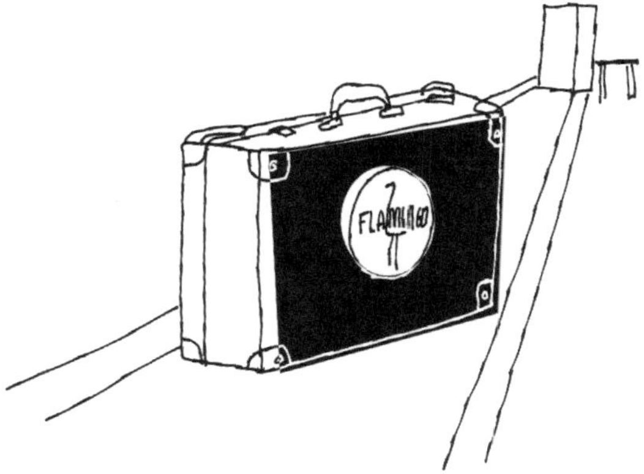
FLAMINGO

SHOP AT JERRY'S MARKET

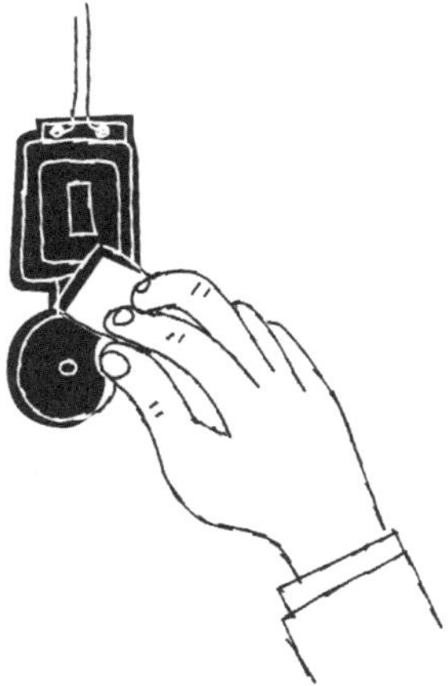

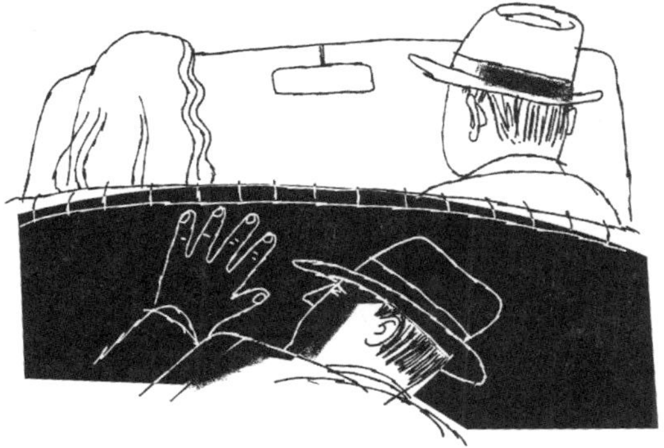

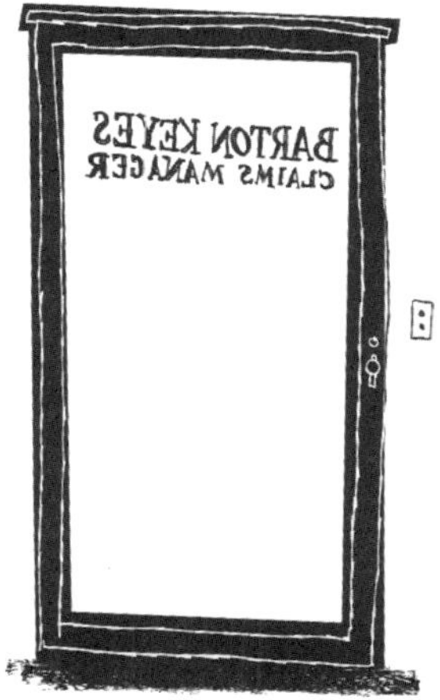
BARTON KEYES
CLAIMS MANAGER

26

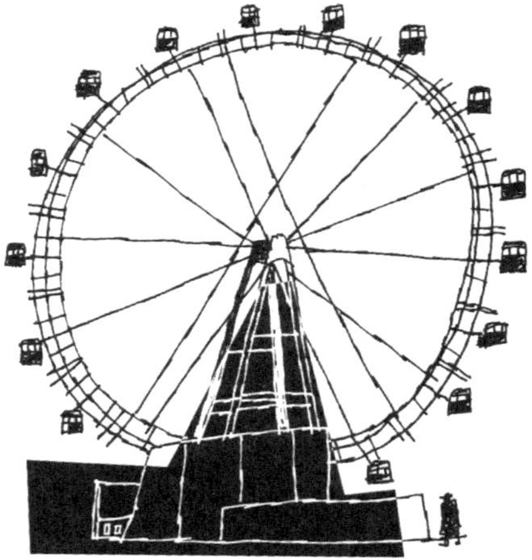

CAFE MARC AUREL

27

DEBONAIR
SOCIAL CLUB
MEMBERS ONLY

An Evening
WITH
JAKE LA MOTTA
featuring the works
of
PADDY CHAYEFSKY
ROD SERLING
SHAKESPEARE
BUDD SCHULBERG
TENNESSEE WILLIAMS
Tonight

6:00

WPBH 9

The
TIP TOP
CAFE

We better get going if we going to stay ahead of the weather

6:00

29

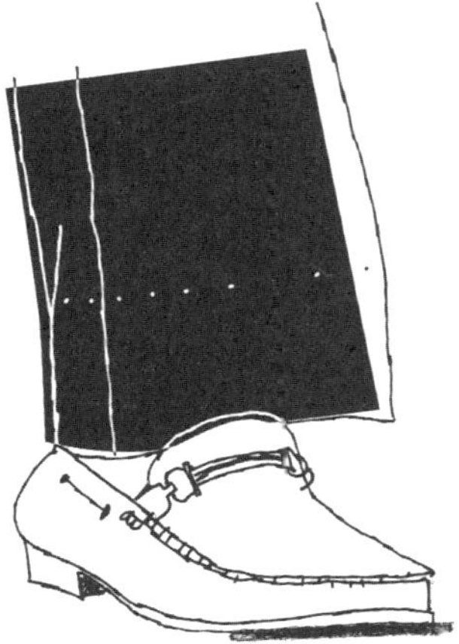

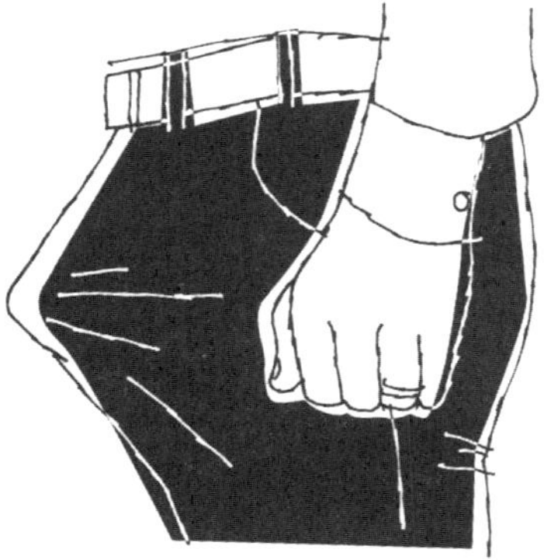

4
KWN
SAN DIEGO
4

NO
TRESPASSING

EL RANCHO
Floor Show
SUSAN ALEXANDER KANE
Twice Nightly

ROSEBUD

31

SOVIC
STUDIOS "LA VICTORINE"

ANTHOLOGIE DU CINEMA
Lubitsch
23
POUR
BUNUEL

JOUR
SONORE
Je vous présente "PAMELA"
FERRAND
Chef Operateur
W. WILLIAM
24
2

PAMELA

CITIZEN KANE
CITIZEN KANE

DEFENSE D' AFFICHER

32

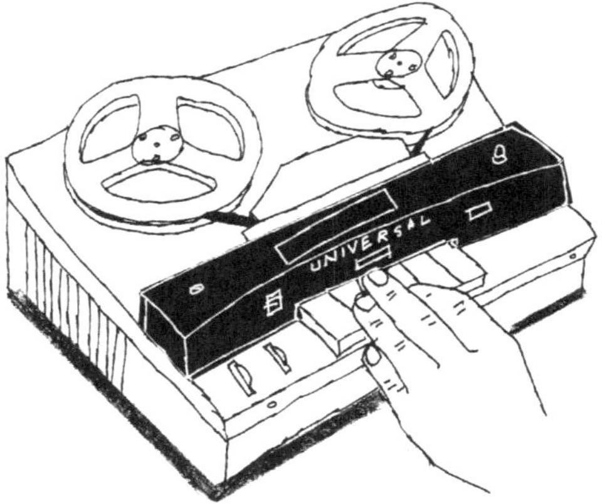

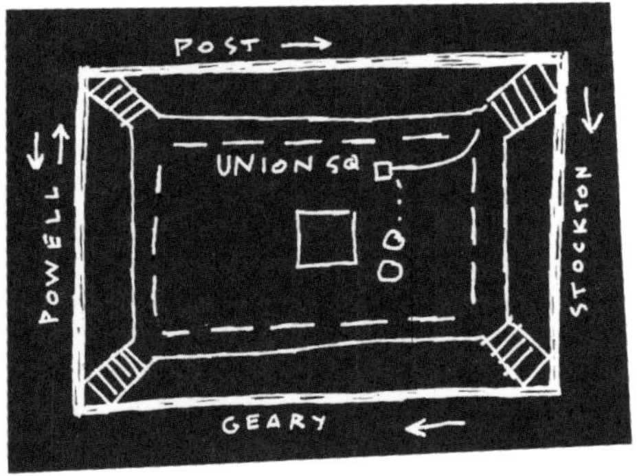
POST
POWELL
STOCKTON
GEARY
UNION SQ

ACTIVE MEMBER
MEMBER

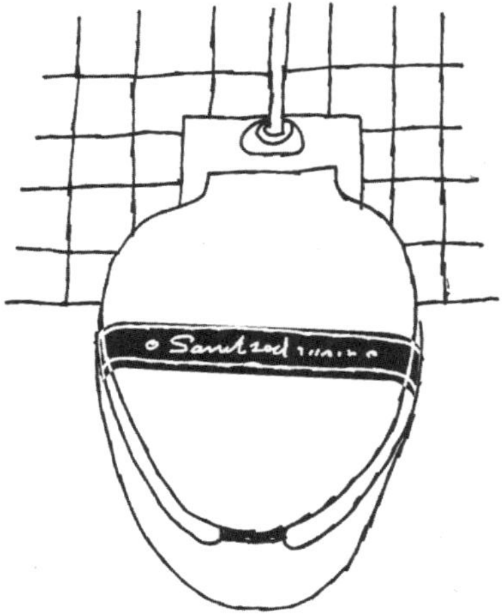

33

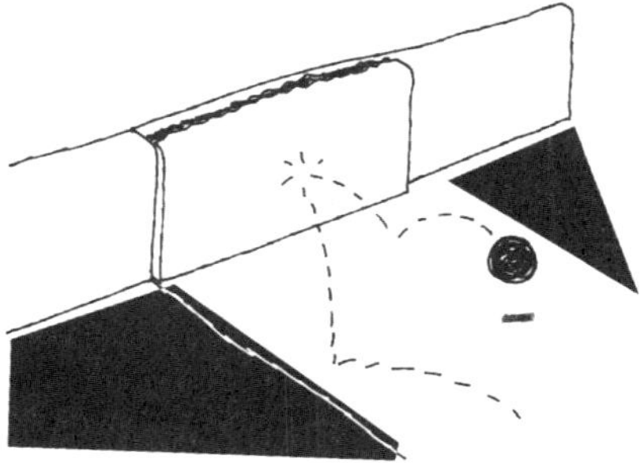

OÙ
& QUAND
OÙ
& QUAND

4
20

34

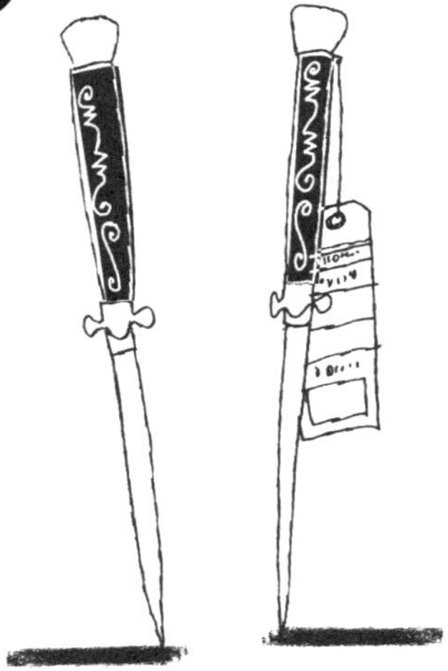

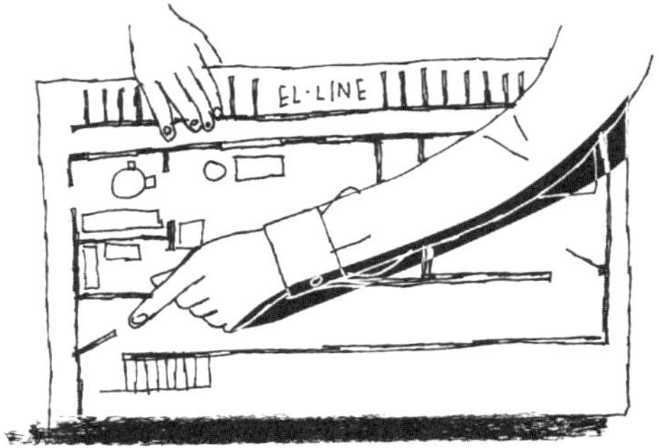

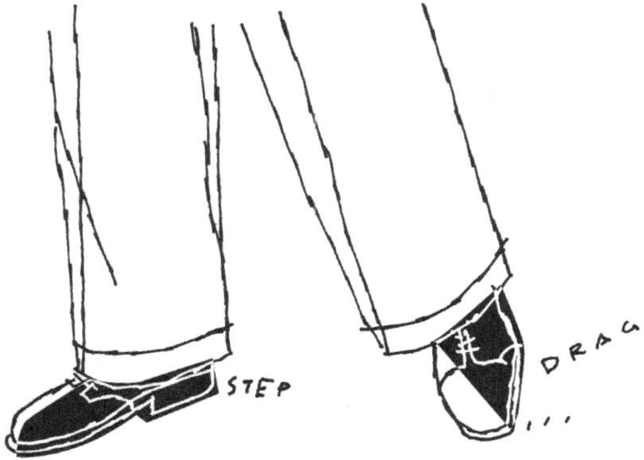
STEP
DRAG
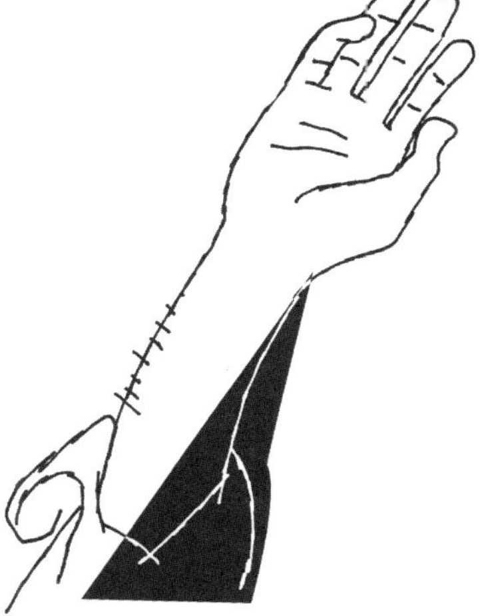

35

STERNWOOD

A.G. Geiger
RARE BOOKS
AND
DE LUXE EDITIONS

DRIVE
LAVERNE TERRACE
BANG!
BANG!
SLAM!

R
Randall Arms
RANDALL
ARMS

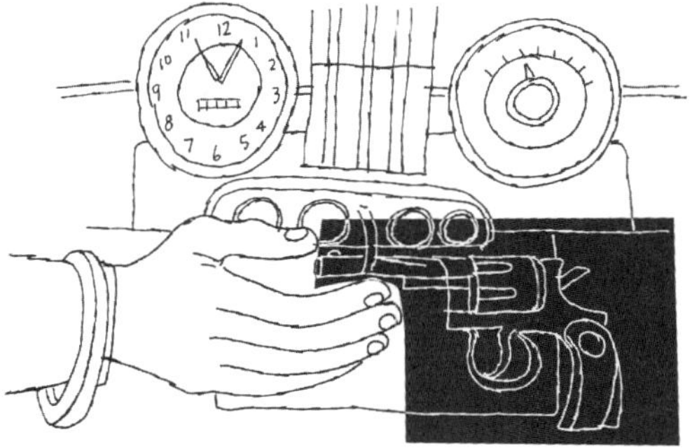

GO WITH THE
GLOBE

SIDNEY FALCO
PUBLICITY

The Elysian
Room

21

J.J. Hunsecker
Get Harry Kells Tonight

ONE WAY
NO TURNS
BUS STOP

37

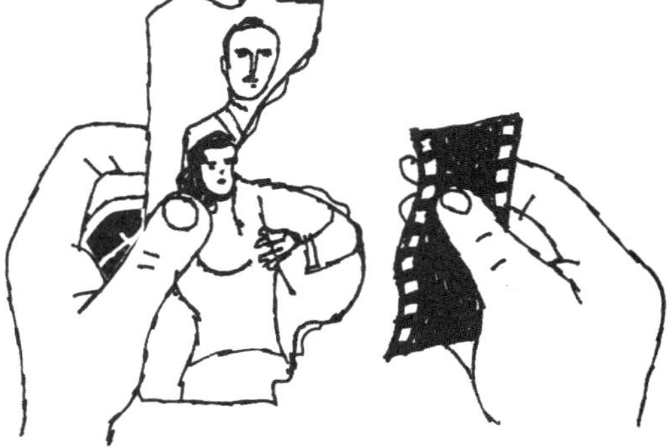

PA ADISO

38

La Louisane

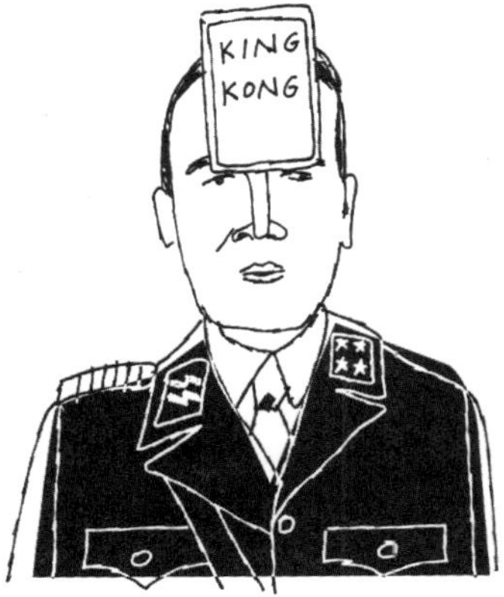
KING
KONG

Für Max,
alle Liebe
Bridget von Hammersmark

39

Elaine's

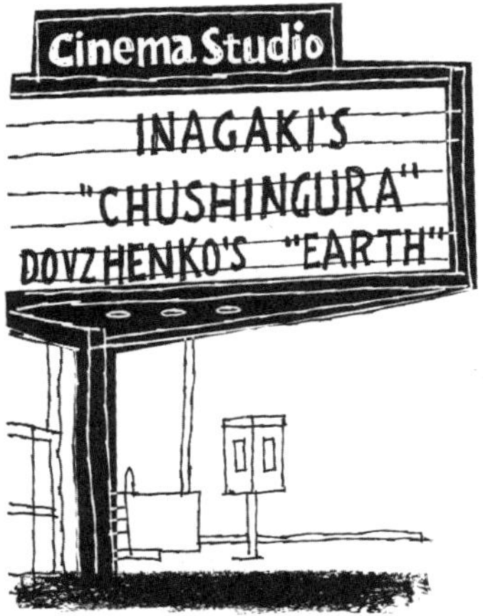
Cinema Studio
INAGAKI'S
"CHUSHINGURA"
DOVZHENKO'S "EARTH"

Marriage Divorce, and Selfhood
Jill Davis
Marriage Divorce, and Selfhood
Jill Davis

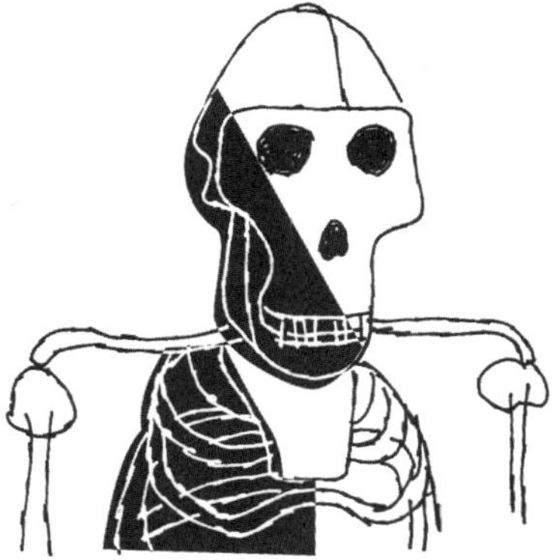

40

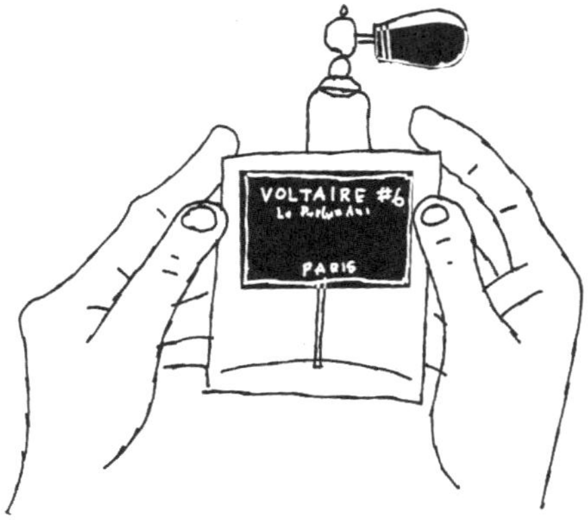

TRANSMISSIONS
ENGINE
SHOCK
SPRING
Luftwaffe Automotive
Specialists in Fine German Motor Cars
30-56

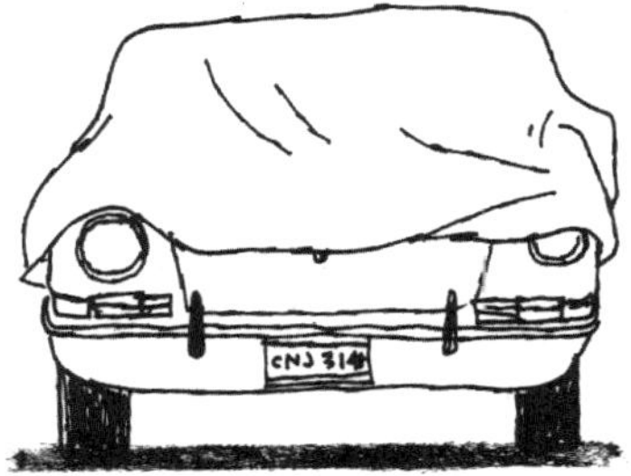

41

GASOLINE
DANGER
1 US GAL

STOP

42

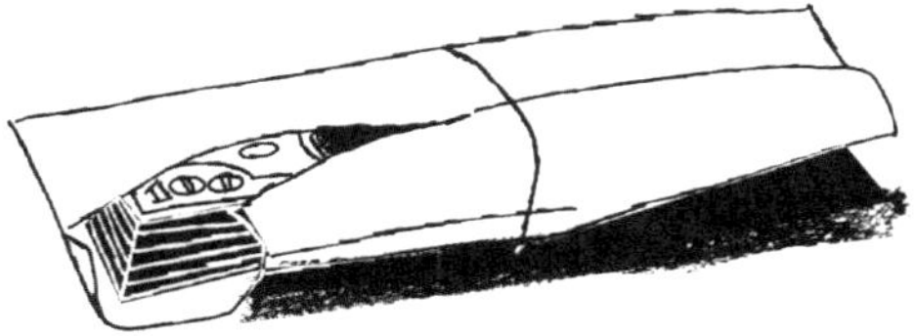

NFB418

DIME AND SPY
INCORPORATED
SIDNEY KIDD
EDITOR AND PUBLISHER

CLICK

PUBLIC LIBRARY
OPEN DAILY
9 AM to 5 PM
WED. EVENINGS
7 PM to 8 PM

C.K. DEXTER HAVEN!

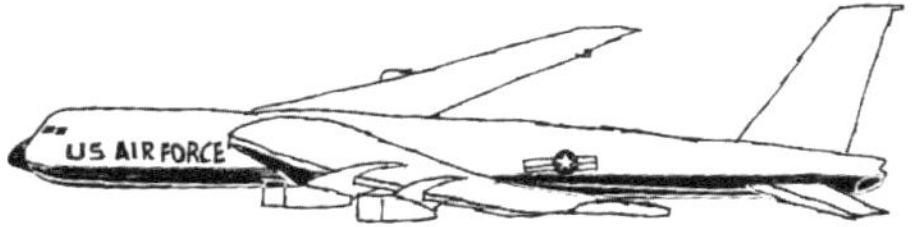
US AIR FORCE

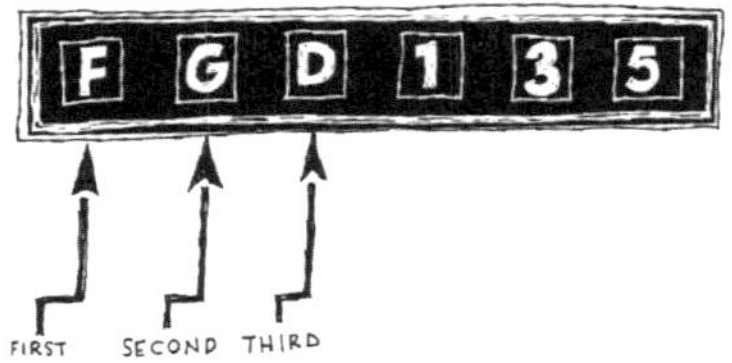
F G D 1 3 5
FIRST
SECOND
THIRD

STRATEGIC AIR COMMAND
BURPELSON AIR FORCE BASE
UNITED STATES AIR FORCE
Peace IS OUR PROFESSION
STOP
STOP

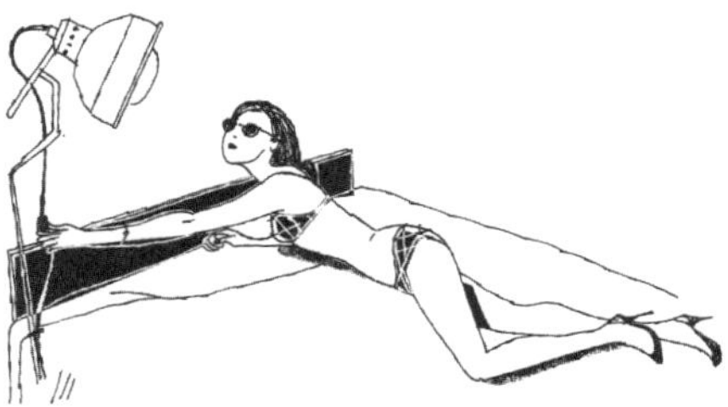

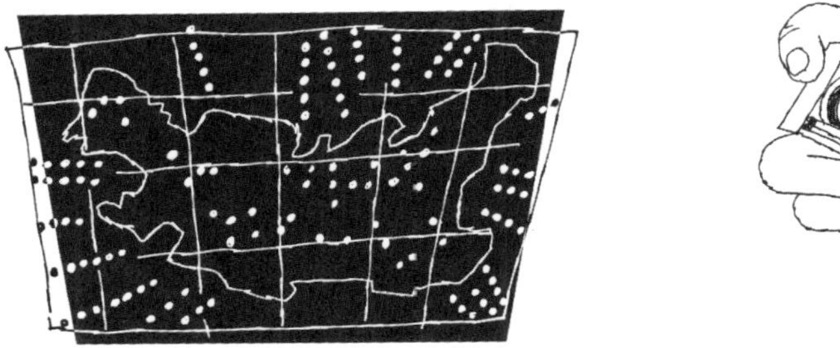

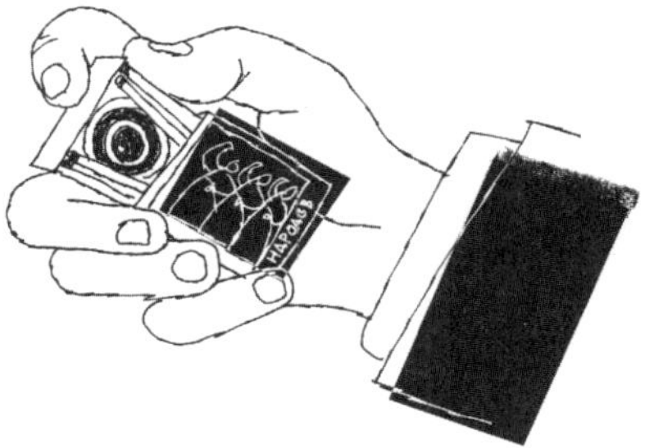
НАРОДОВ

STATE PRISON
30265
Ellis Boyd Redding/30265
Determination
REJECTED

His Judgement Cometh
and that Right Soon....

Ellis
MEXICO

46

NOT TOO LOUD!
THE NEIGHBORS
ARE COMPLAINING

THE MUSIC MAN
ONE OF THE BEST MUSICAL COMEDIES OF OUR TIMES"

C. C. BAXTER
2nd ADMINISTRATIVE
ASSISTANT

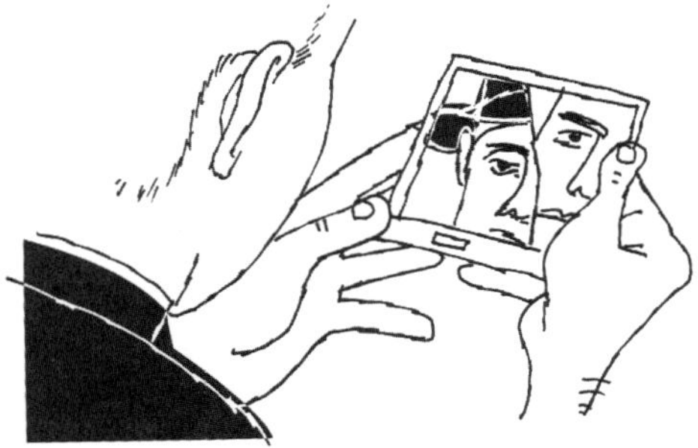

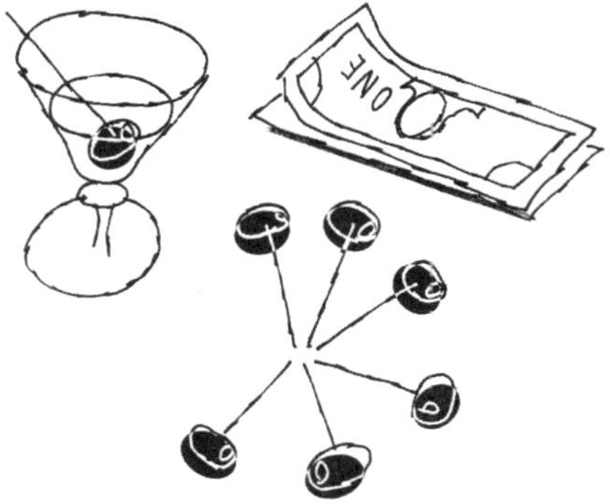
ONE

SLEEP

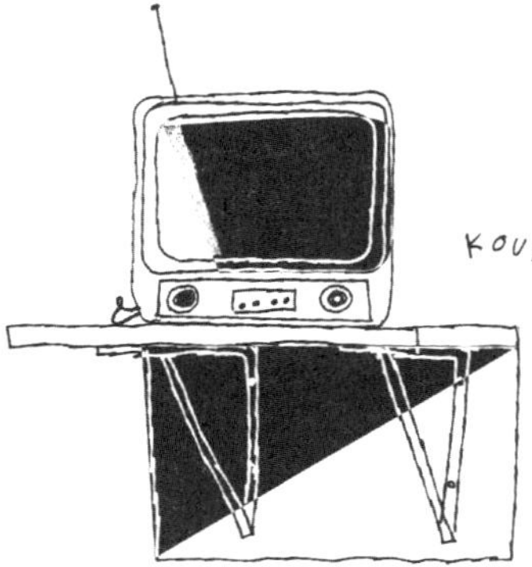

KOUFAX INTO HIS WIND-UP

CHARTER BOATS
BAIT

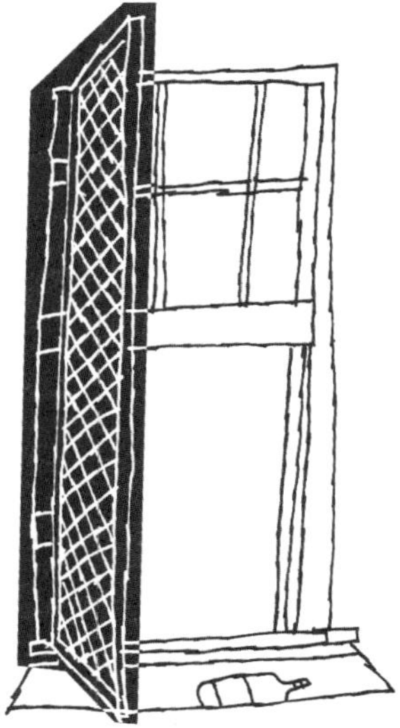

BOOKENDS SIMON & GARFUNKEL

A
Continental HYATT HOUSE

STILLWATER

ROLLING STONE
Stillwater Runs Deep!
by William Miller

49

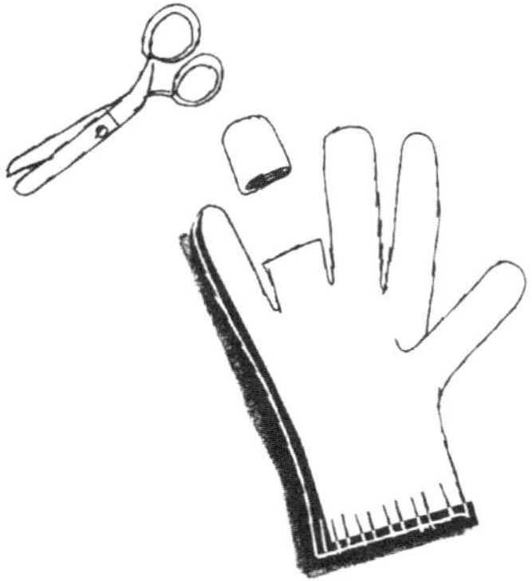

U-BOAT
NAVAL GAME
MB
ingame
RISK
PARKER BROTHERS
Clue
APH
Tri-Ominos
MB
BINGO
SCRABBLE

375th STREET Y
BUS

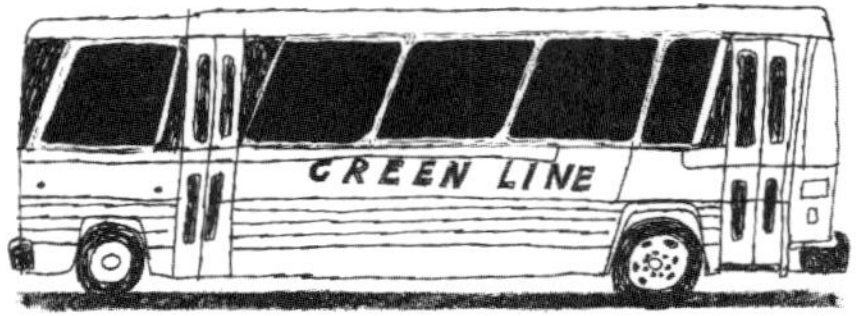
GREEN LINE

50

BIG TEX DRIVE IN

NEW YORK
Luxury Liner
NATIONAL
300

this is me

MUTUAL OF NEW YORK

MIAMI

51

The
END

SPECIAL

ION CARD
PICTURES INC.
JOHN L. SULLIVAN
DEPT. Director
Jan. 2, 1941
1941

WEATHER
Kansas City Tribune
LATEST NEWS
STRANGE DEATH OF HOLLYWOOD DIRECTOR
PROMINENT CITIZENS ALONG WITH CIVIC BODIES COMBINE TO MAKE CITY PARK SUCCESS
Accord Reached Farm Payments
JOHN L. SULLIVAN FOUND DEAD IN FREIGHT YARDS

O BROTHER WHERE ART THOU?
BY
Sinclair Beckstein

WMAL

LATEST NEWS
WEATHER
Washington Chronicle
'MAN FROM MARS' ESCAPES
Eludes Military During Walkout From Army Hospital
Review of the News

Yellow Cab
Co.
LAwrence
64212

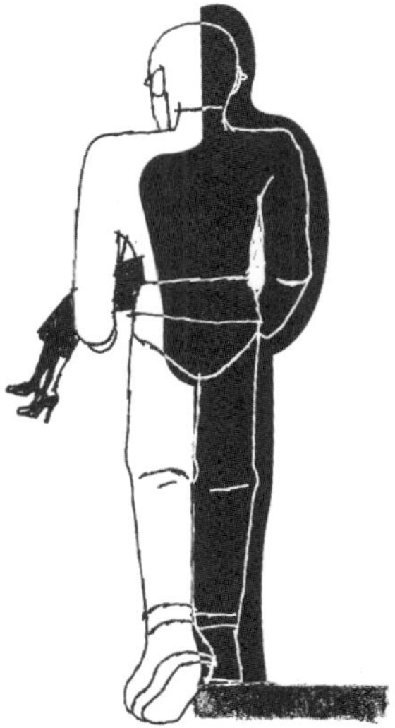

53

San Francisco Post-Dispatch
THURSBY, ARCHER MURDERS LINKED
CONSERVATIVES HALT CONFIRMATION MOVE
FEDERAL R REPORTS CHANGES
Private Detective Was Shadowing Thursby.

PASSPORT
Joel Cairo

SHIPPING NEWS
Arriving Today
5:35 P.M – La Paloma from Hong Kong
6:20 P.M.–Shasta King from Seattle

PRIVATE

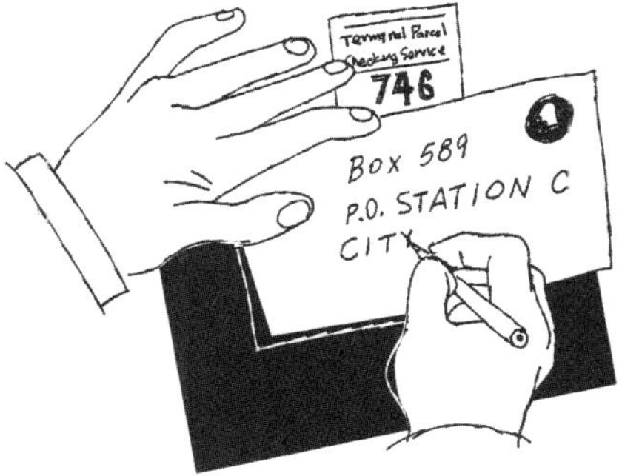
Terminal Parcel
Checking Service
746
Box 589
P.O. STATION C
CITY

MONUMENTAL
PICTURES

MOUNT
HOLLYWOOD
ART SCHOOL

GRAUMANS
CHINESE
PREMIERE TONIGHT
BIGGEST PICTURE OF 1927
DON LOCKWOOD-LINA LAMONT
IN
THE ROYAL RASCAL

STAGE
BROADWAY
SREEN
VARIETY
25 CENTS
STUDIOS CONVERT TO TALKIES
BEST RESTAURANT ON B'WAY STARTS ON SHOESTRING
MAD SCRAMBLE ON FOR SOUND
SOCK BIZ FOR LEGIT NOW - BUT MOVIES STILL STIFF

VOWEL E

HOTEL
ASTOR
STRAND
SARDIS
Casino
PALACE
Gaiety
LOEW'S
LOEW'S STATE
TOR HOTEL
CRITERION

WE LOVE
WAKE UP CLUB
FM 108
FM 108
WE LOVE

NY

NEW YORK POST
PHEW!
Hazy, hot humid and headed toward 100°

BED STUY

Sal's
SPECIAL CALZONE 2.99

JOEYS
COOP

25 MEN

57

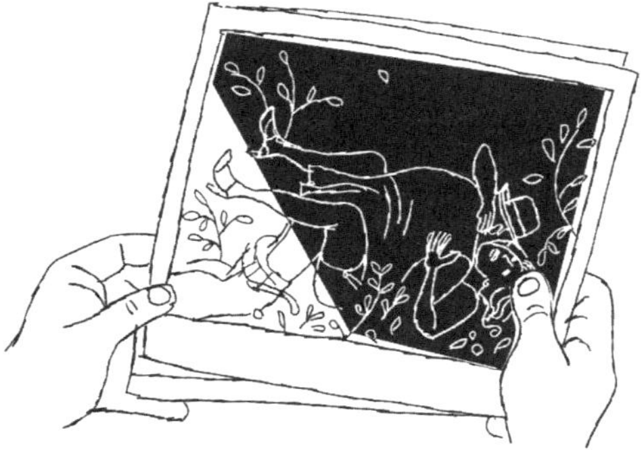

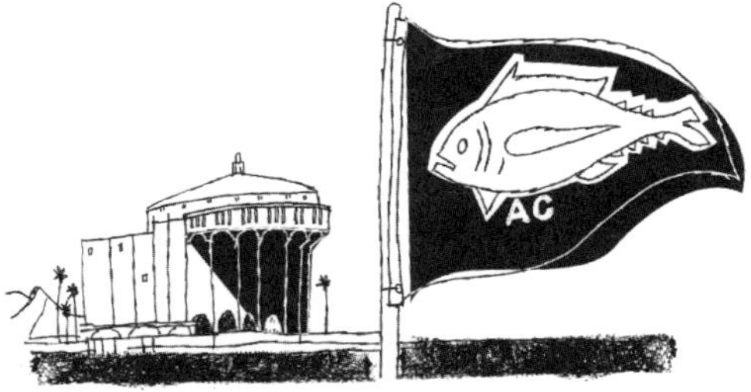
AC

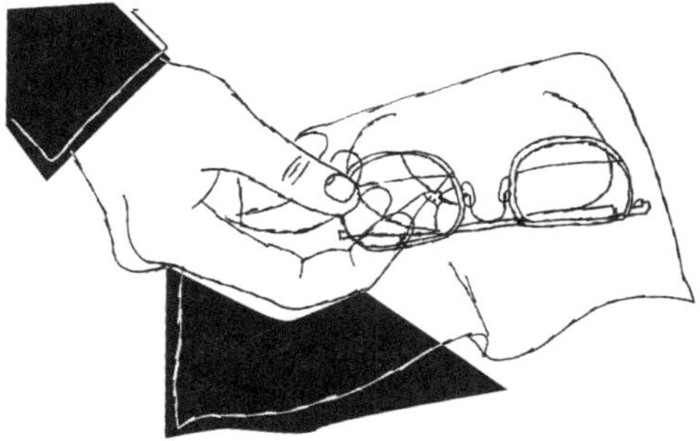

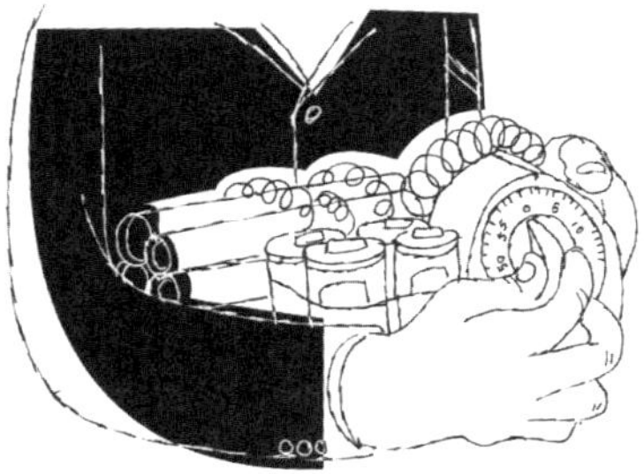

HOTEL
ENTRANCE

ZITA
THIS WEEK ONLY

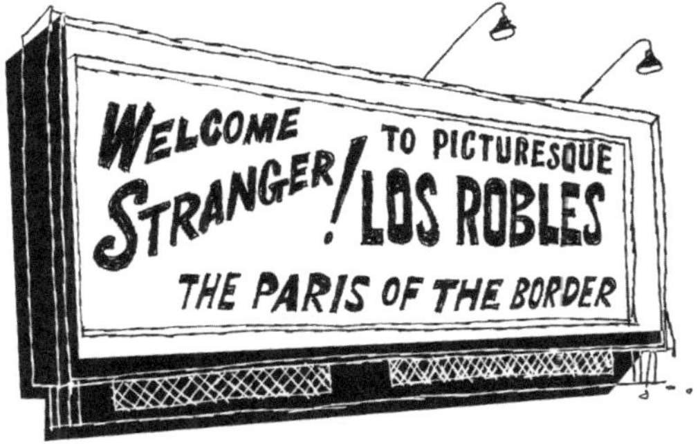
WELCOME STRANGER!
TO PICTURESQUE
LOS ROBLES
THE PARIS OF THE BORDER

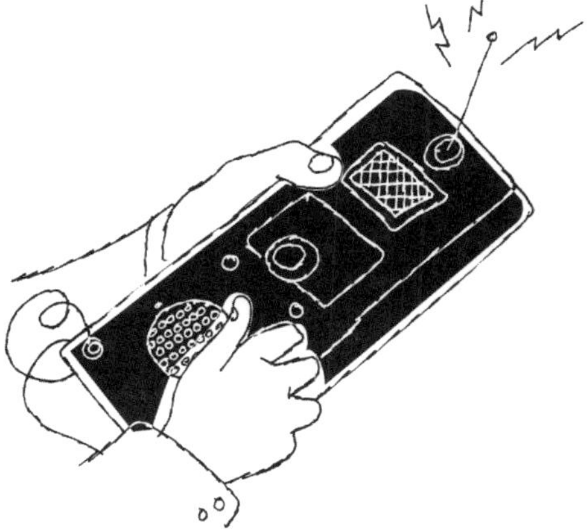

59

Paris-flirt
GAPTE • HUMOR • FANTASIE

NEW YORK
Herald Tribun

Plus dure
sera
la chute
ROD STEIGER • JAN STERLING
CETTE SEMAINE

STAGE

MERCURY
MERCURY THEATRE

THEATRE NATIONAL
OPERA
BALLET LERMONTOV
GISELLE HEART OF FIRE
LA BOUTIQUE FANTASQUE

GOV

YES
NO

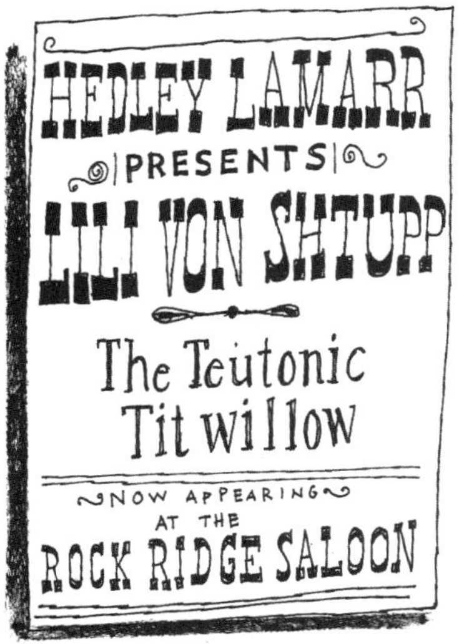
HEDLEY LAMARR
PRESENTS
LILI VON SHTUPP
The Teutonic
Tit willow
NOW APPEARING
AT THE
ROCK RIDGE SALOON

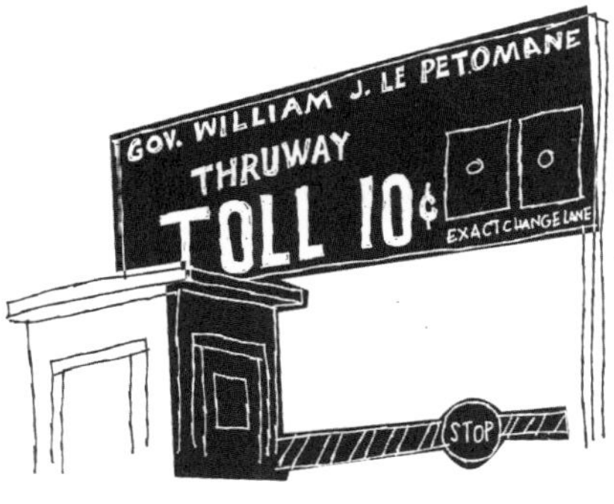
GOV. WILLIAM J. LE PETOMANE
THRUWAY
TOLL 10¢
EXACT CHANGE LANE
STOP

ALTO
NIDO
6550

Rx
Schwab's
PHARMACY
TOILET
ARTICLES
8024
PRESCRIPTIONS
DRUGS
Breakfast
Luncheon Dinner
Prescriptions
Free Delivery

Paramount Pictures

Mad about the Boy. Norma

63

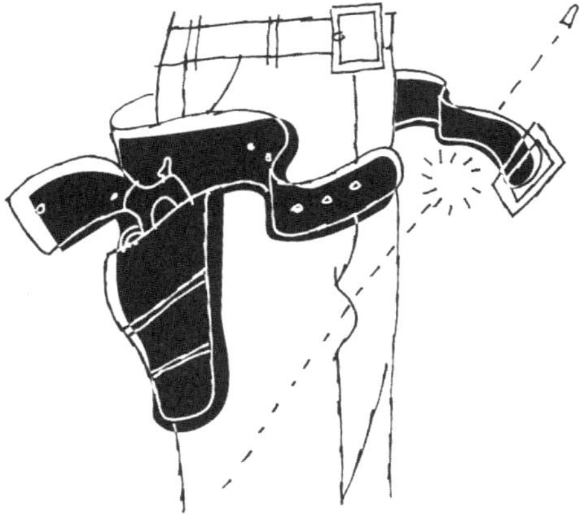

NEW YORK TRAVEL
COMPANY
STEAMSHIP
Passage to
South America

NACIONAL

BANDIDOS YANQUIS
BANDIDOS DE LOS ESTADOS UNIDOS

64

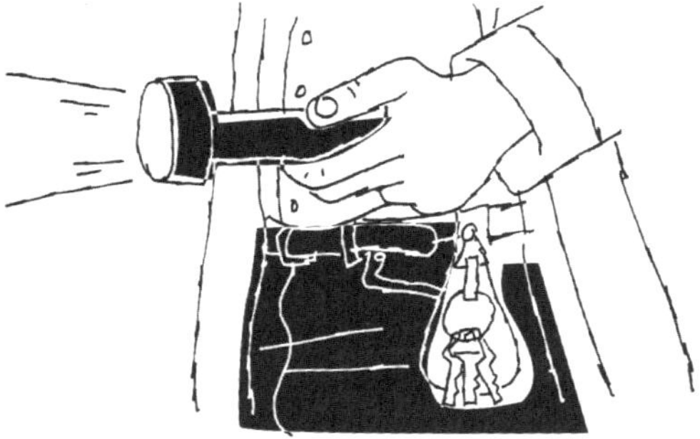

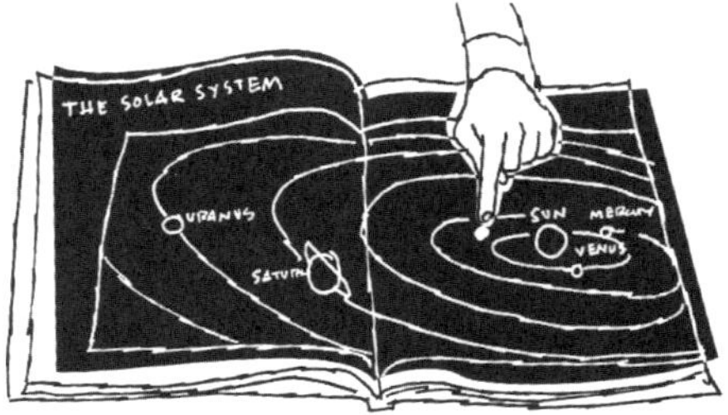

SUBWAY

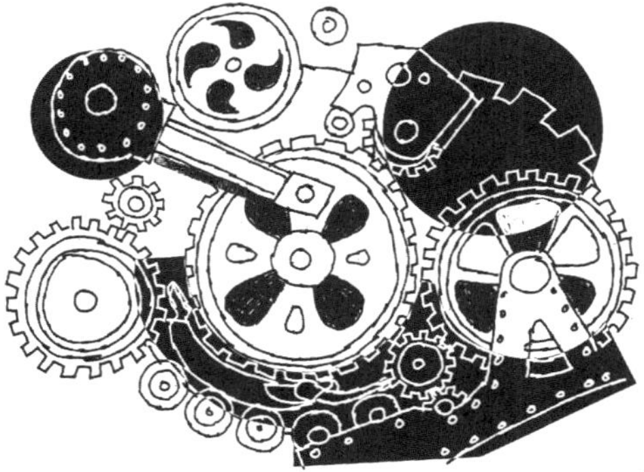

EXTRA
THE DAILY NEWS
STRIKES AND RIOTS!
BREADLINES BROKEN BY UNRULY MOB

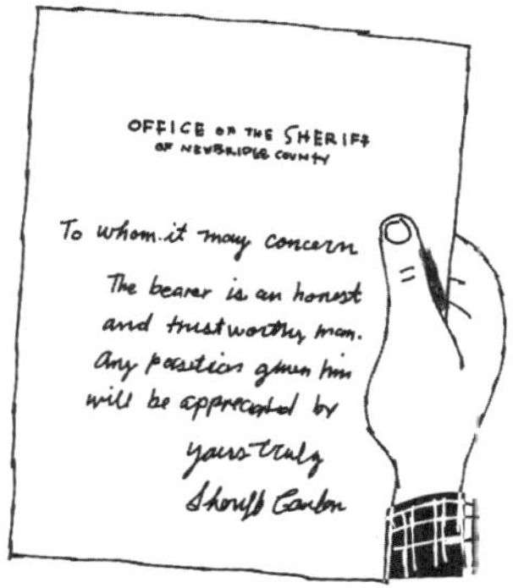
OFFICE OF THE SHERIFF
OF NEWBRIDGE COUNTY
To whom it may concern
The bearer is an honest and trustworthy man. Any position given him will be appreciated by
Yours truly
Sheriff Carlson

a pretty girl and a gay old man
flirted on the boulevard
he was a fat old thing
but his diamond ring
caught

66

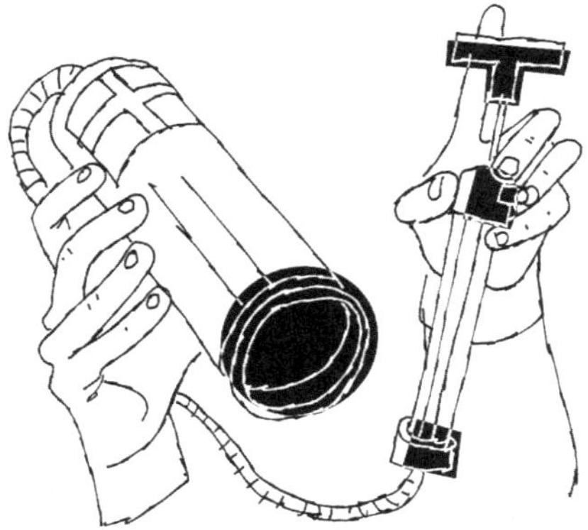

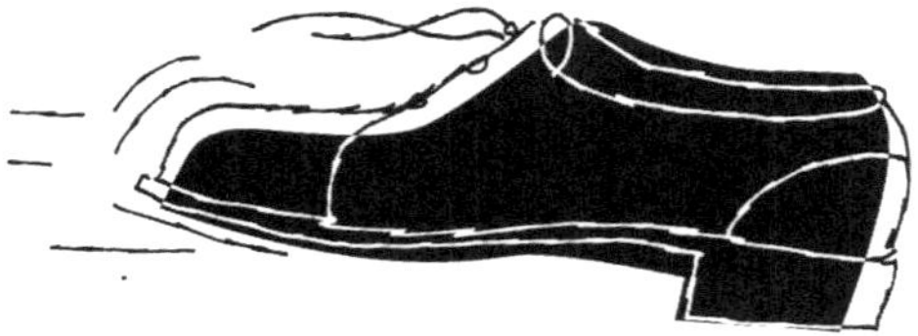

R
PEOPLE I KNOW
JIMI HENDRIX DECEASED
JANIS JOPLIN
MAMA CASS

Hot
Trax

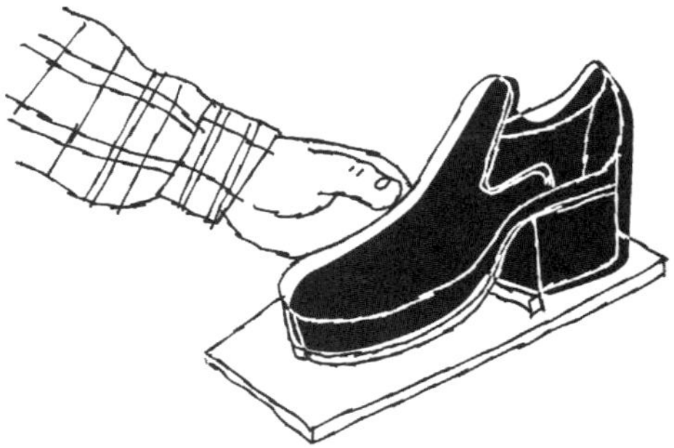

68

DON'T LEAVE
THE HOUSE
TODAY

Chuck's
BIKE-O-RAMA

MADAM RUBY'S
TAROT
CARDS
INCOME TAX
PALMS
READ

69

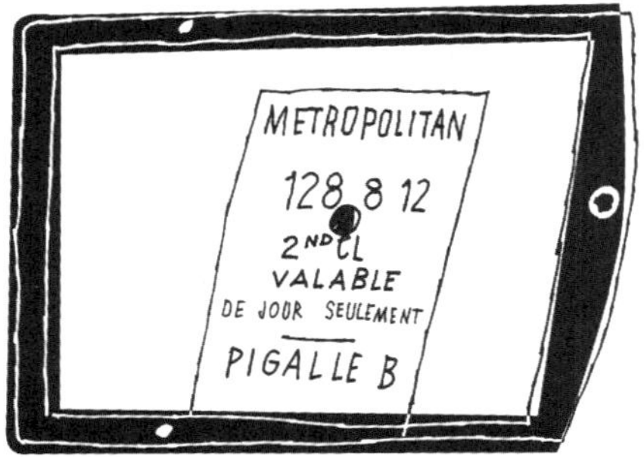
METROPOLITAN
128 8 12
2ND CL
VALABLE
DE JOUR SEULEMENT
PIGALLE B

0
10
20
30
40
50
60
70

EXPLOSIVES

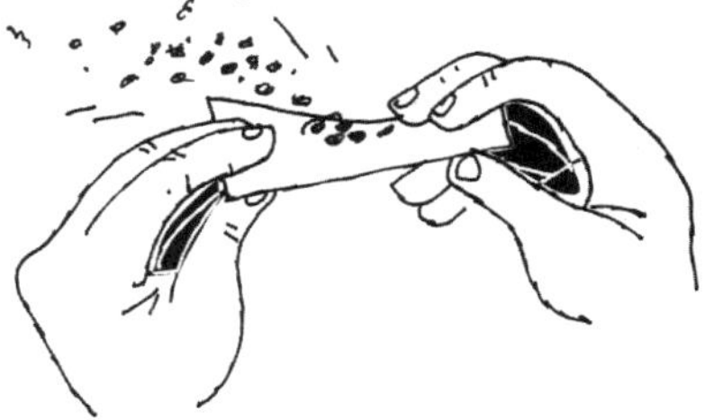

70

EIGENTUM
DER
DEUTSCHEN
WERRMAGAT

WH-112Q4

TOP SECRET
ARMY INTEL 990633
DO NOT OPEN

71

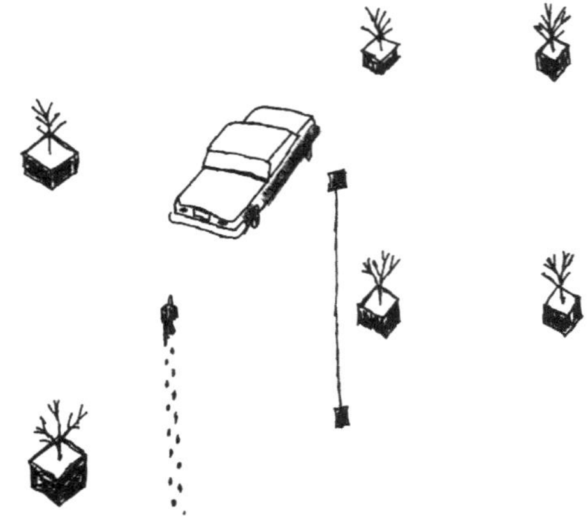

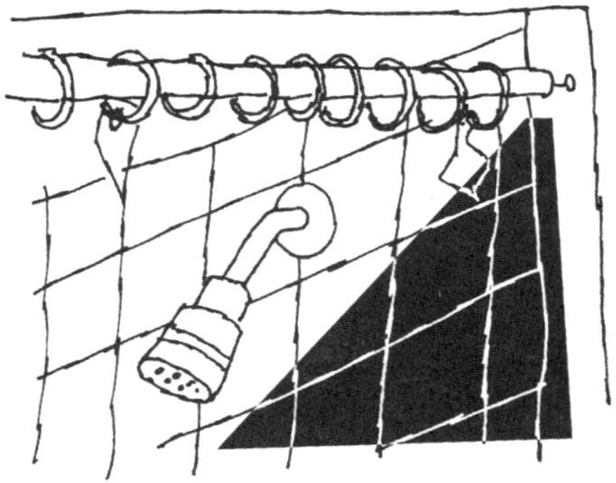

Lakeside Club
POLICE

Carlton
Celebrity Room
In Person
JOSE FELICIANO
Limited Engagememt
Feb. 3-5 9 pm

EMIL FABER
FOUNDER - AD 1904
KNOWLEDGE IS GOOD

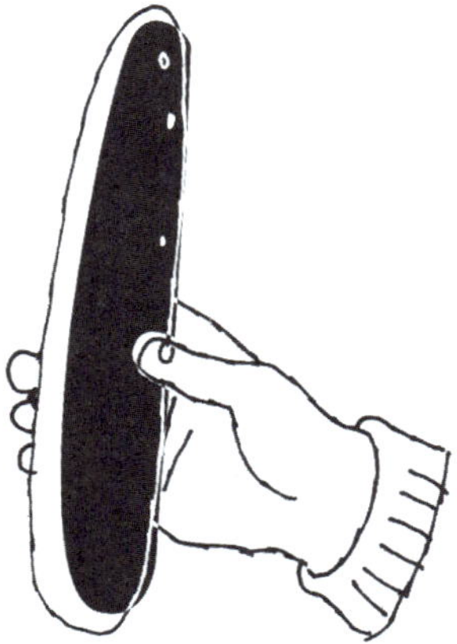

OTIS
DAY
& THE
KNIGHTS

MOTEL
Rainbow
VACANCY

Eat Me

73

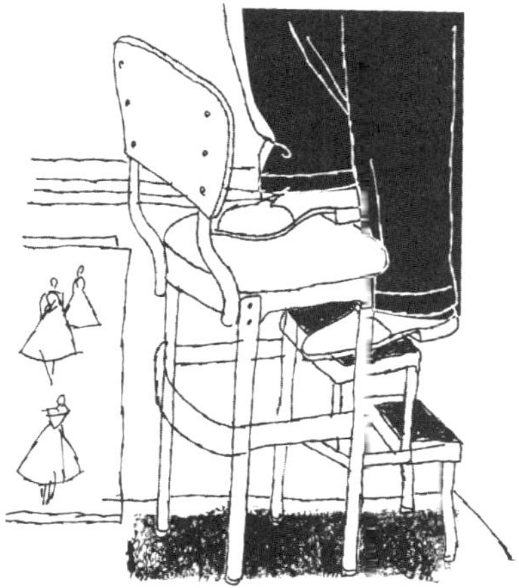

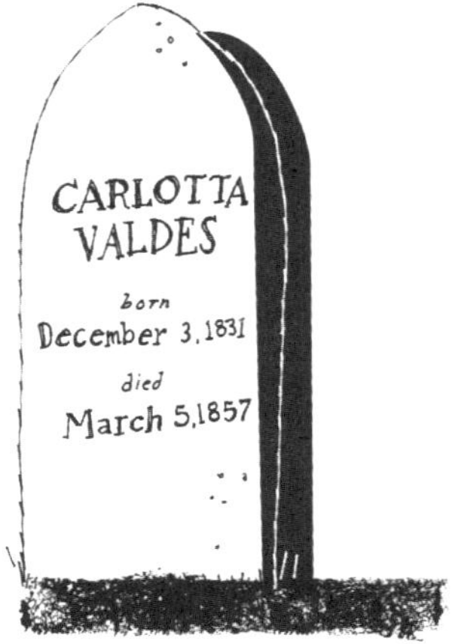

HOTEL EMPIRE
EMPIRE HOTEL

74

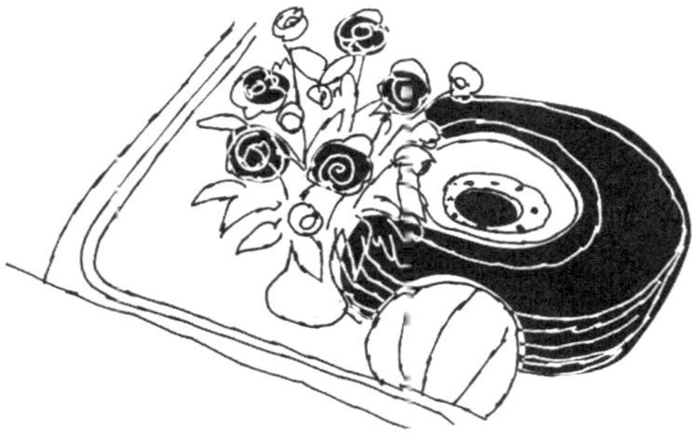

PRICK

75

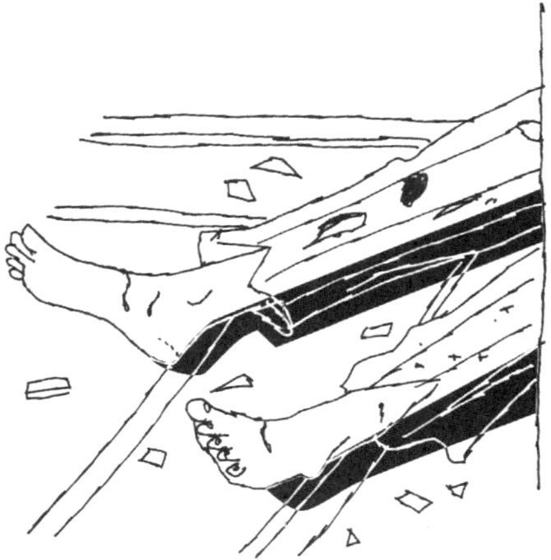

CAPITOL
OIL Co.
LUBRICATION
TIRES · BATTERIES
BODEGA BAY SERVICE
TIRE SALE

76

BARBER

SEMINOLE RITZ
HOTEL

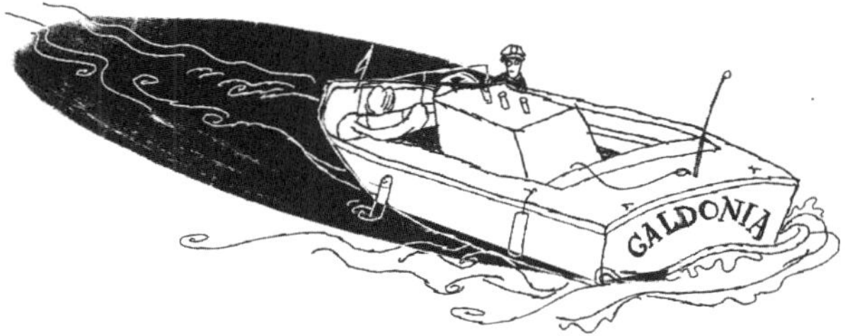
CALDONIA

RITZ

CARNIVAL
SEMI-GLOS

2001 ODDYSSEY
PRESENTS
Fr Sat CAROL DOUGLAS
WITH BLUE MAGIC
2001 ODDYSSEY
2001
ODYSSEY
ANNUAL DISCO
DANCE CONTEST
GRAND PRIZE $500

1301
Phillips
DANCE
Studio
DOWNSTAIRS

278
Verrazano
Narrows Br
Staten Island
New Jersey
PAY TOLL 2 1/2 MILES

TROJANS
TROJANS
TROJANS

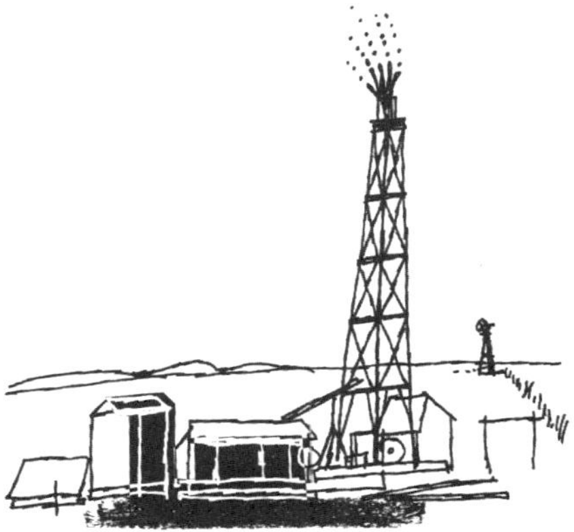

BENEDICT

JR

WE RESERVE
THE RIGHT
TO REFUSE SERVICE
TO ANYONE

WELCOME HOME MICHAEL

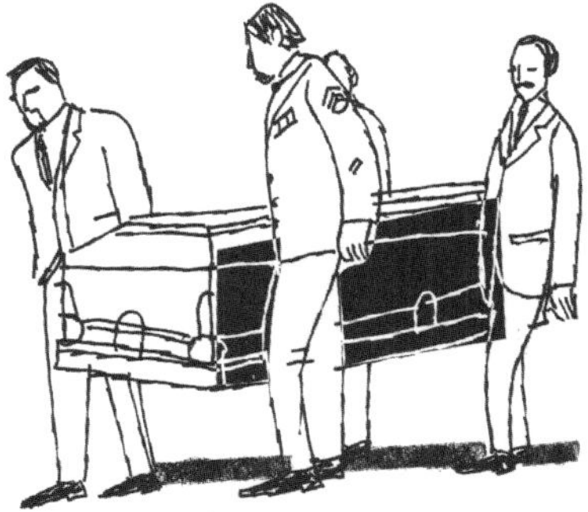

THE SORROW
AND
THE PITY
©CINEMA 5 LTD. 1972
©MARCEL OPHULS, ANDRE HARRIS. 1969

100 FPI
NEW YORK

TAIL OF THE PUP
TAIL OF THE PUP
La Cienega Bl

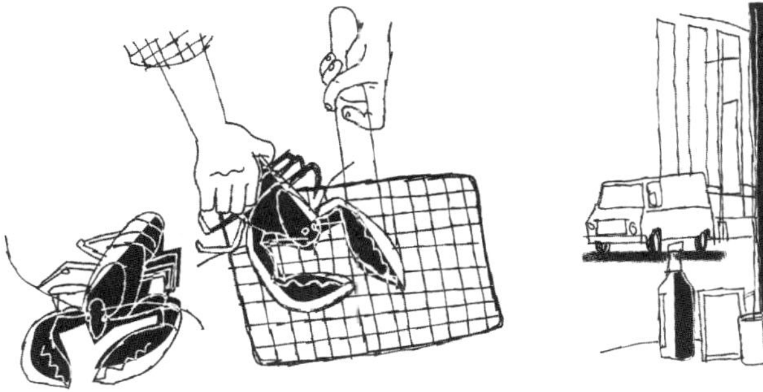

W 63rd
WALK

Chez Luis

WRIGLEY FIELD
HOME OF
CHICAGO CUBS
SAVE
FERRIS
THIS BUDS FOR YOU

HOWE
9

SMITHS
3017

83

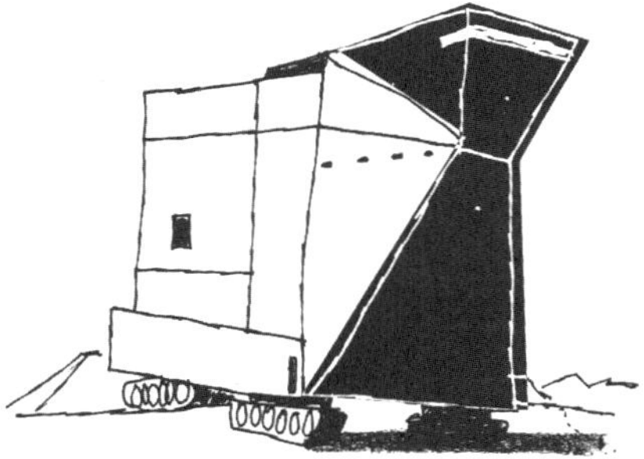

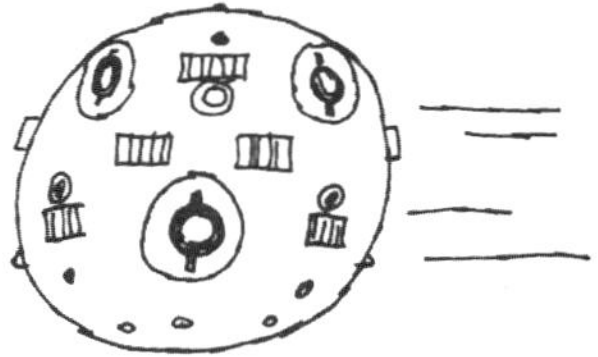

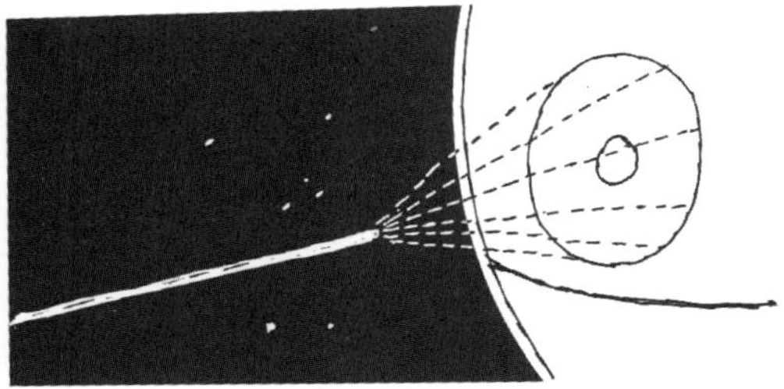

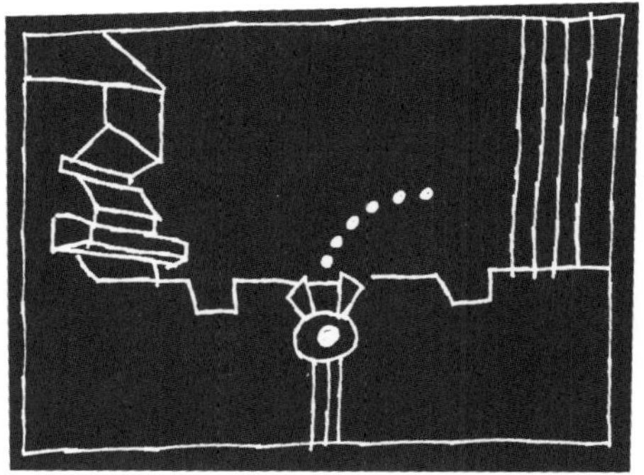

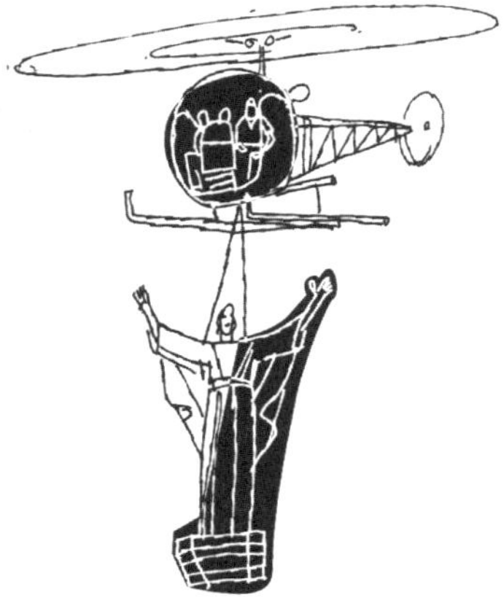

acqua
S.PELLEGRINO

85

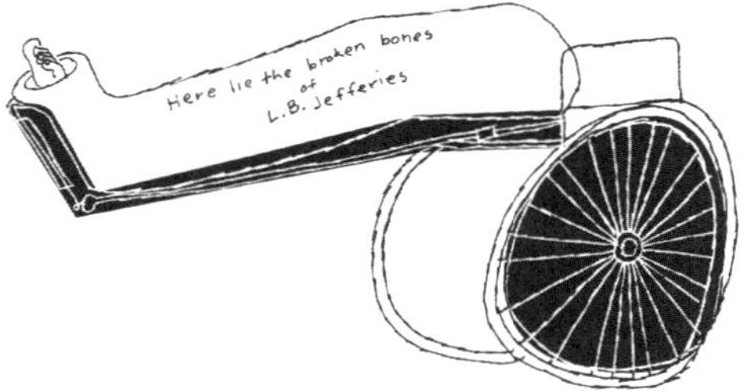

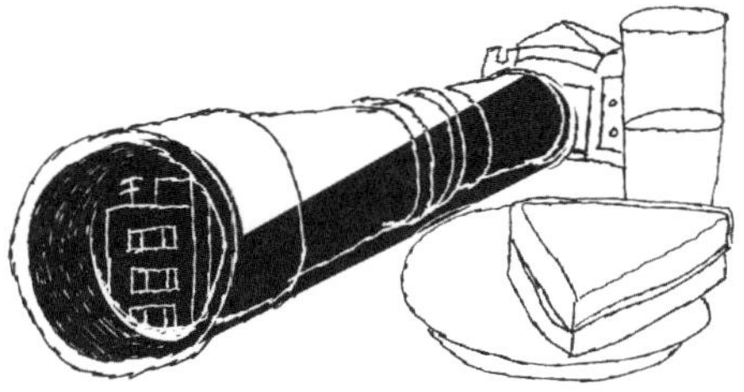

VIDEO DIFFICULTIES
are TEMPORARY
Please
do not adjust
your set.
UBS
UBS

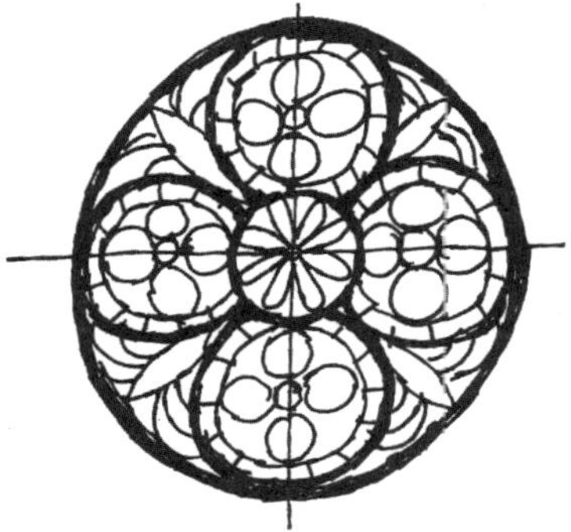

Why compromise?
Yuban
Yuban
Yuban

55
AMERICAN
LITERARY
HISTORICAL
SOCIETY

CIA
123
123

378 HFN

Times
10:39
The

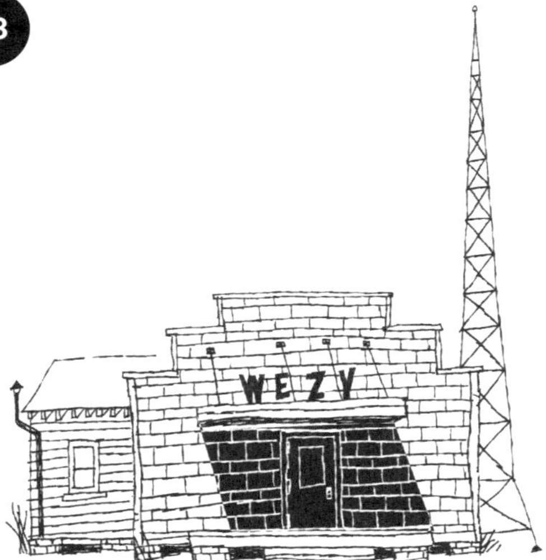
WEZY

K141

BOSTONIANS
Shoes for Men

HOMER STOKES
FRIEND of the LITTLE MAN
OUR NEXT
GOVERNOR

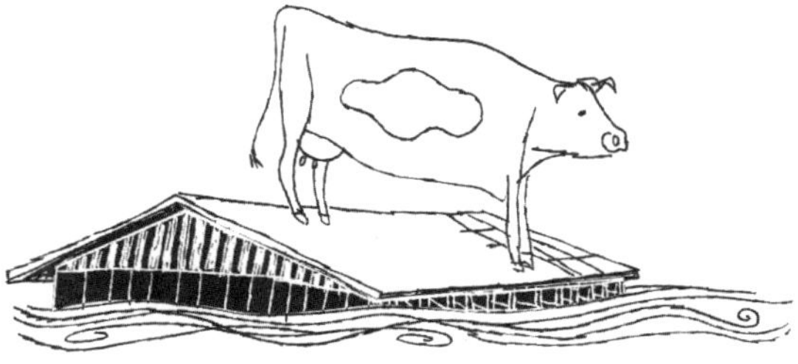

89

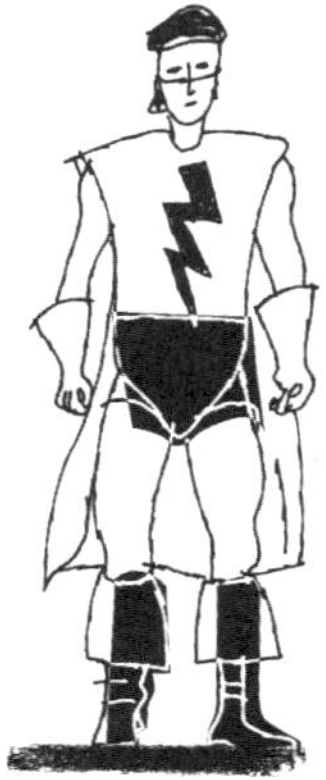

K37 496

LIUM

Carnegie DELICATESSEN
RESTAURANT
854

90

NATIONAL
BOHEMIAN
Fells Point

91

BLENDED
WHISKEY
TIMES
CARS
WAIT
WALK

RACING

HELP
YOURSELF
BROTHER!
SAVE A SOUL
MISSION
SAVE A SOUL

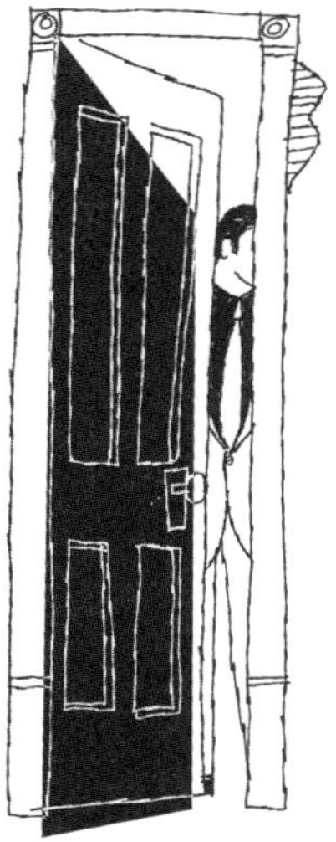

Hav'na Drink
RESTAURANT
Mindys

The BOOK of THE FILM

CAMELOT 43
CAMELOT 43
CAMELOT 43
CERTIN DEATH 1
CERTIN DEATH 1
CERTIN DEATH 1

93

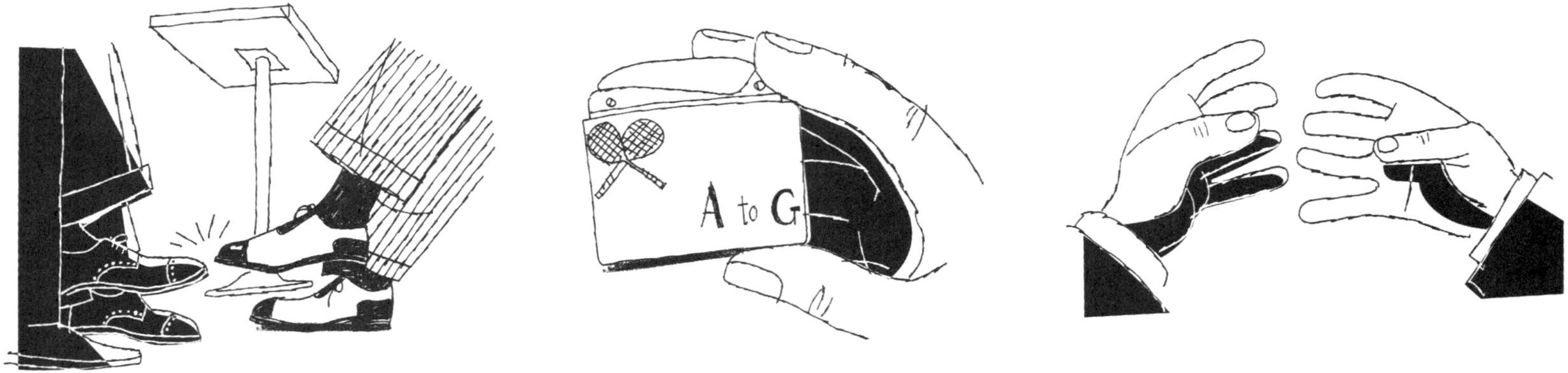

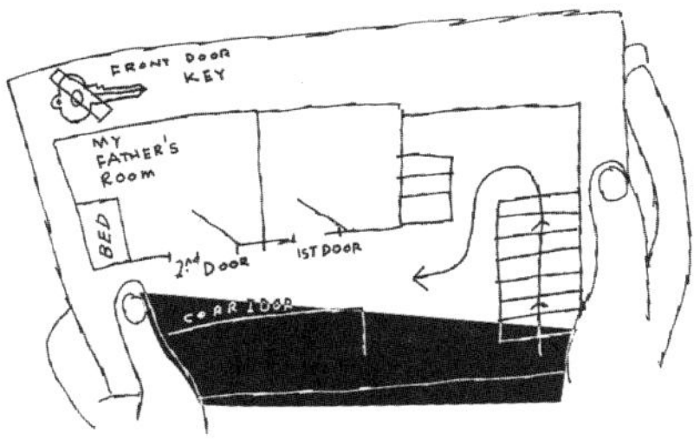
FRONT DOOR
KEY
MY FATHER'S ROOM
BED
2nd DOOR
1ST DOOR
CORRIDOR

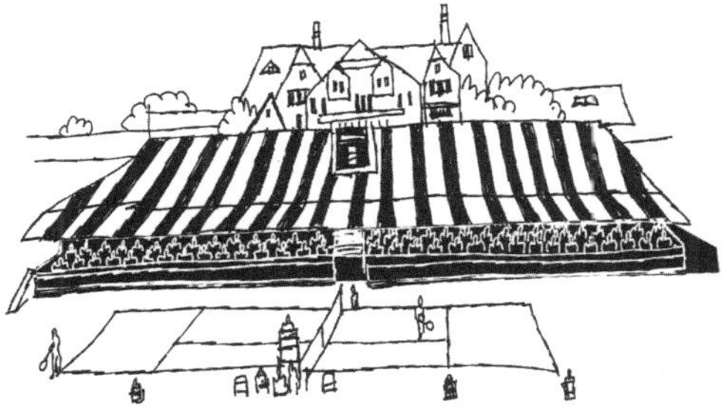

CRAFTS
20 BIG
SHOWS

94

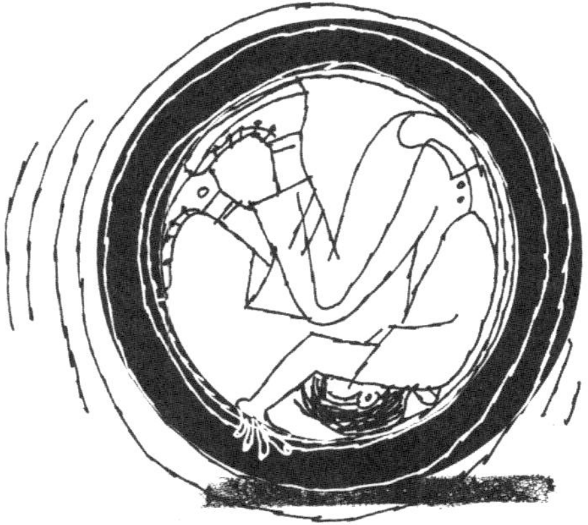

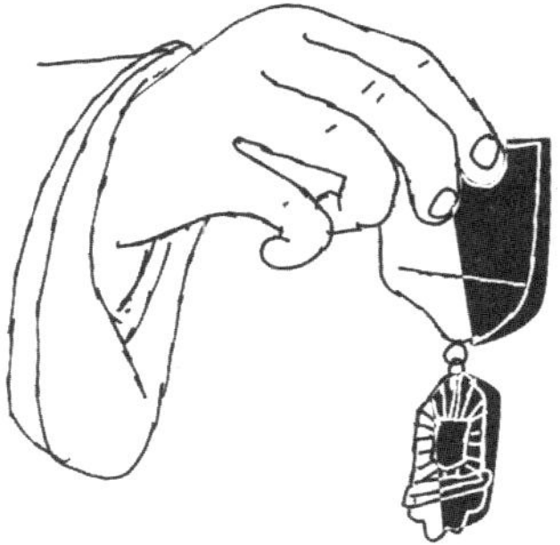

HAM

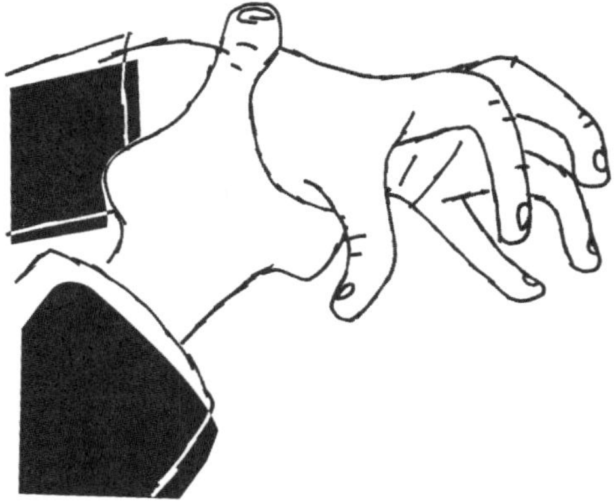

95

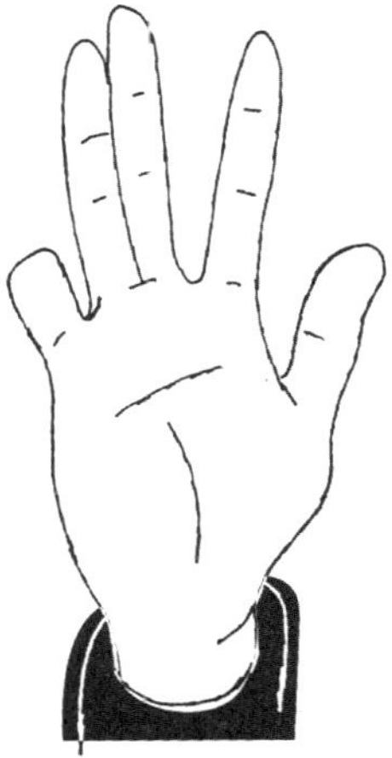

To John
from Margaret
The Lord bless thee
and keep thee
Easter 1928
THE CHURCH HYMNAL
REVISED EDITION

PALLADIUM
CRAZY MONTH

DETTE
GARAGE DU PORT-AUBIN
CHRYSLER

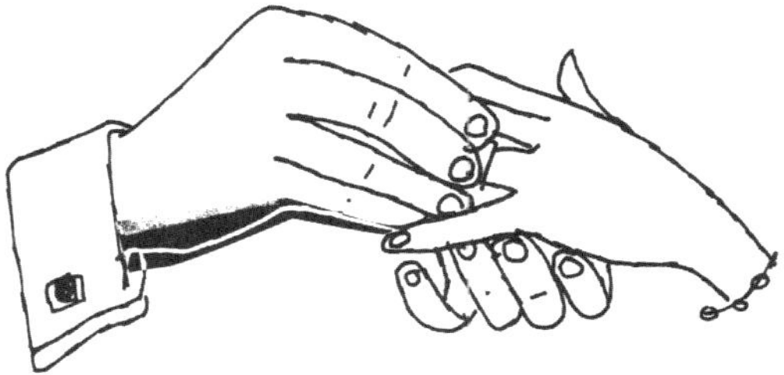

Mme Eme

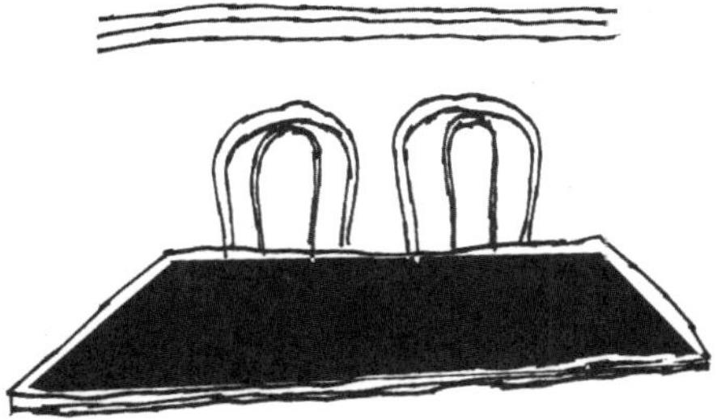

ESSO
ESSO SERVICE
L'ESCALE CHERBOURGEOISE

97

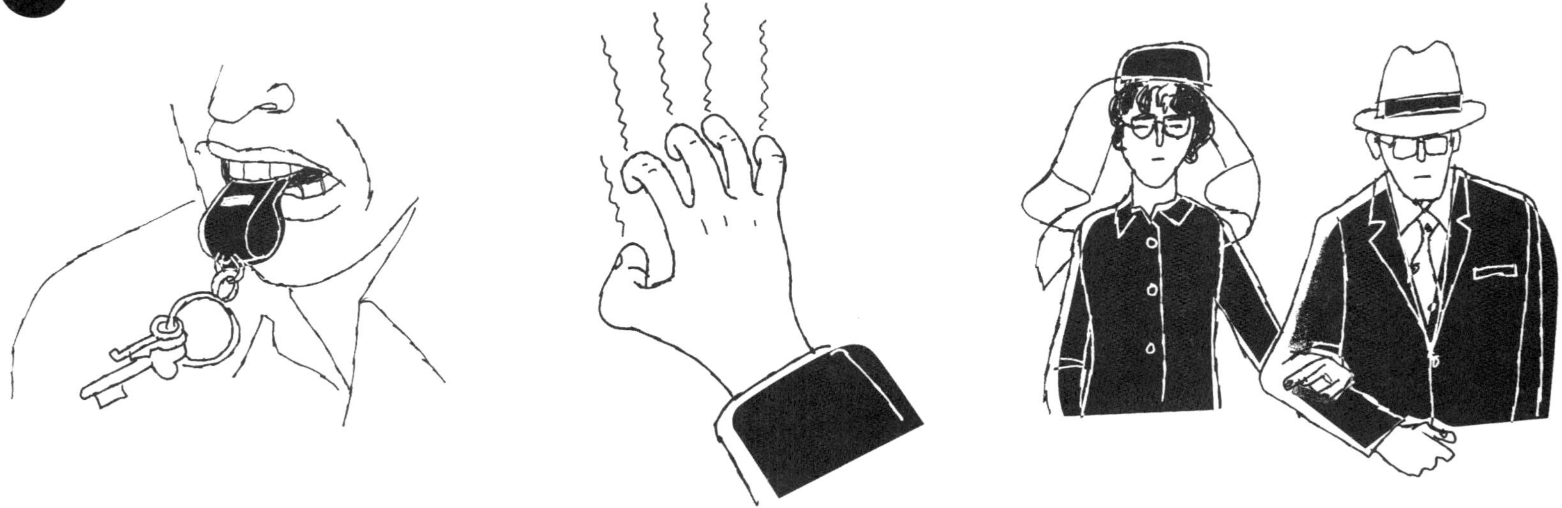

SPORTSMENS PARADISE
72 LOUISIANA
73

ORCA

CHET!

Hotel EARLE
"A DAY OR A LIFETIME"
Hotel EARLE

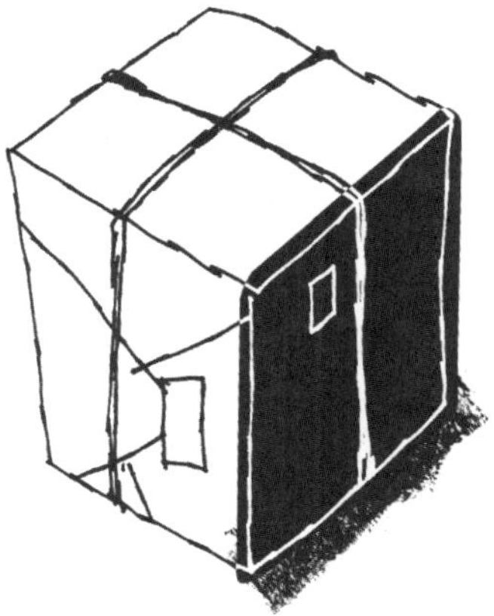

99

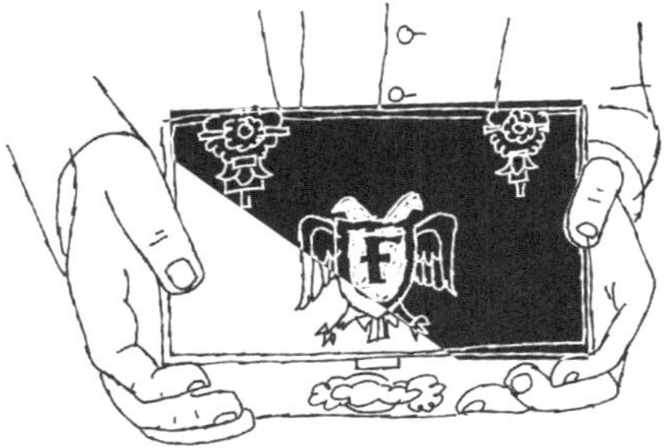

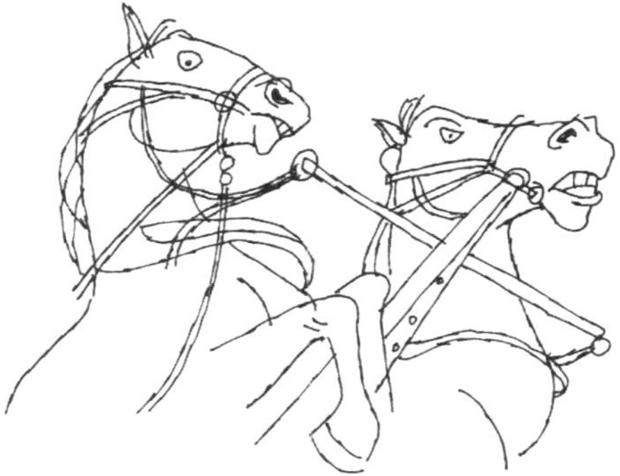

3 Years Dead

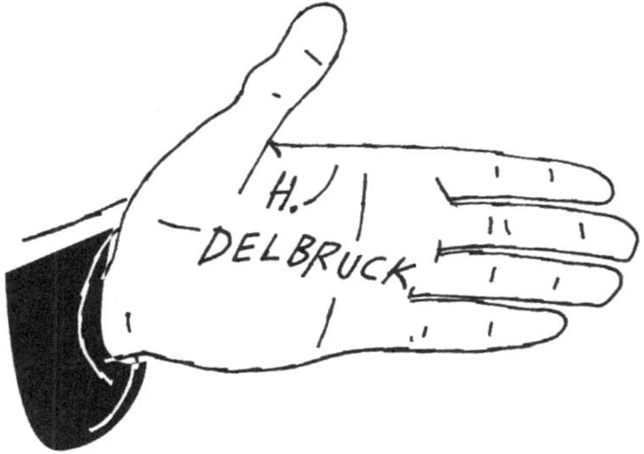
H. DELBRUCK

Bucharest Academy of Science
TONIGHT ONLY
DR. F. FRANKENSTEIN
PRESENTS
THE CREATURE
IN
"A Startling New Experiment in
PRESENTED IN
(Transylvania
SOLD OUT

PROFESSOR
MARVEL
ACCLAIMED BY
The CROWNED HEADS of EUROPE
LET HIM READ YOUR
PAST • PRESENT and FUTURE
IN HIS CRYSTAL
also JUGGLING and SLEIGHT OF HAND

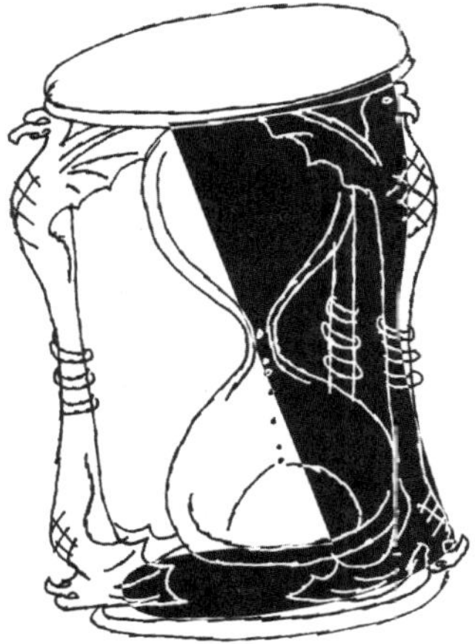

STATE
FAIR
OMAHA

SOLUTIONS

1 Casablanca (1942)

2 Zoolander (2001)

3 Pulp Fiction (1994)

4 Titanic (1997)

5 Bonnie and Clyde (1967)

6 Le Parrain
The Godfather (1972)

7 Very Bad Trip
The Hangover (2009)

8 L'Arnaque
The Sting (1973)

9 Kill Bill Vol. 1 (2003)

10 The Big Lebowski (1998)

11 Bullitt (1968)

12 Les Affranchis
Goodfellas (1990)

13 Taxi Driver (1976)

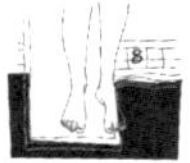

14 La Dernière Séance
The Last Picture Show (1971)

15 Cent dollars pour un shérif
True Grit (1969)

16 Clerks : les employés modèles
Clerks (1994)

17 Le facteur sonne toujours deux fois
The Postman Always Rings Twice (1946)

18 La Mort aux trousses
North by Northwest (1959)

19 Le Lauréat
The Graduate (1967)

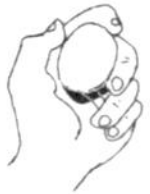

20 Luke la main froide
Cool Hand Luke (1967)

21 Le Tambour
Die Blechtrommel (1979)

22 Le Roman de Mildred Pierce
Mildred Pierce (1945)

23 Les Arnaqueurs
The Grifters (1990)

24 L'Ultime Razzia
The Killing (1956)

25 Assurance sur la mort
Double Indemnity (1944)

26 Le Troisième Homme
The Third Man (1949)

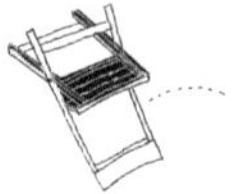

27 Raging Bull (1980)

28 Un jour sans fin
Groundhog Day (1993)

29 Présentateur vedette : la légende de Ron Burgundy
Anchorman: The Legend of Ron Burgundy (2004)

30 Citizen Kane (1941)

31 La Nuit américaine (1973)

32 Conversation secrète
The Conversation (1974)

33 Le Fabuleux Destin d'Amélie Poulain (2001)

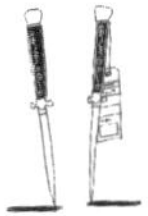

34 Douze hommes en colère
12 Angry Men (1957)

35 Le Grand Sommeil
The Big Sleep (1946)

36 Le Grand Chantage
Sweet Smell of Success (1957)

37 Cinema Paradiso
Nuovo cinema Paradiso (1988)

38 Inglourious Basterds (2009)

39 Manhattan (1979)

40 À bord du Darjeeling Limited
The Darjeeling Limited (2007)

41 Reservoir Dogs (1992)

42 Psychose
Psycho (1960)

43 Indiscrétions
The Philadelphia Story (1940)

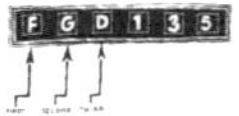

44 Docteur Folamour (1964)
Dr. Strangelove (1964)

45 Les Évadés
The Shawshank Redemption (1994)

46 La Garçonnière
The Apartment (1960)

47 Vol au-dessus d'un nid de coucou
One Flew Over the Cuckoo's Nest (1975)

48 Presque célèbre
Almost Famous (2000)

49 La Famille Tenenbaum
The Royal Tenenbaums (2001)

50 Macadam Cowboy
Midnight Cowboy (1969)

51 Les Voyages de Sullivan
Sullivan's Travels (1941)

52 Le jour où la terre s'arrêta
The Day the Earth Stood Still (1951)

53 Le Faucon maltais
The Maltese Falcon (1941)

54 Chantons sous la pluie
Singin' in the Rain (1952)

55 Do the Right Thing (1989)

56 Sur les quais
On the Waterfront (1954)

57 Chinatown (1974)

58 La Soif du mal
Touch of Evil (1958)

59 À bout de souffle (1960)

60 Les Chaussons rouges
The Red Shoes (1948)

61 Le shérif est en prison
Blazing Saddles (1974)

62 Boulevard du crépuscule
Sunset Blvd. (1950)

63 Butch Cassidy et le Kid
Butch Cassidy and the Sundance Kid (1969)

64 E.T., l'extra-terrestre
E.T.: The Extra-Terrestrial (1982)

65 Les Temps modernes
Modern Times (1936)

66 Austin Powers
Austin Powers: International Man of Mystery (1997)

67 Boogie Nights (1997)

68 Pee Wee Big Adventure
Pee-Wee's Big Adventure (1985)

69 Le Salaire de la peur
The Wages of Fear (1953)

70 Les Aventuriers de l'arche perdue
Raiders of the Lost Ark (1981)

71 Fargo (1996)

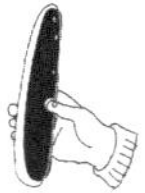

72 American College
Animal House (1978)

73 Sueurs froides
Vertigo (1958)

74 Ça chauffe au lycée Ridgemont
Fast Times at Ridgemont High (1982)

75 Les Oiseaux
The Birds (1963)

76 Un après-midi de chien
Dog Day Afternoon (1975)

77 Certains l'aiment chaud
Some Like It Hot (1959)

78 La Fièvre du samedi soir
Saturday Night Fever (1977)

79 Géant
Giant (1956)

80 Voyage au bout de l'enfer
The Deer Hunter (1978)

81 Annie Hall (1977)

82 La Folle Journée de Ferris Bueller
Ferris Bueller's Day Off (1986)

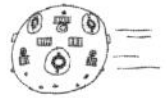

83 Star Wars : Épisode IV – Un nouvel espoir
Star Wars: Episode IV – A New Hope (1977)

84 La Dolce Vita (1960)

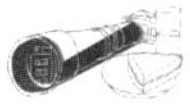

85 Fenêtre sur cour
Rear Window (1954)

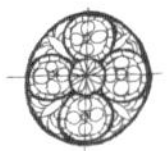

86 Main basse sur la télévision
Network (1976)

87 Les Trois Jours du Condor
Three Days of the Condor (1975)

88 O Brother
O Brother, Where Art Thou? (2000)

89 Broadway Danny Rose (1984)

90 Diner (1982)

91 Blanches colombes et vilains messieurs
Guys and Dolls (1955)

92 Monthy Python : Sacré Graal !
Monty Python and the Holy Grail (1974)

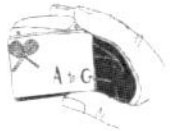

93 L'Inconnu du Nord-Express
Strangers on a Train (1951)

94 Du silence et des ombres
To Kill a Mockingbird (1962)

95 Les Trente-Neuf Marches
The 39 Steps (1935)

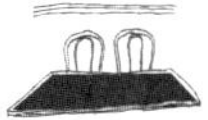

96 Les Parapluies de Cherbourg (1964)

97 Les Dents de la mer
Jaws (1975)

98 Barton Fink (1991)

99 Frankenstein Junior
Young Frankenstein (1974)

100 Le Magicien d'Oz
The Wizard of Oz (1939)

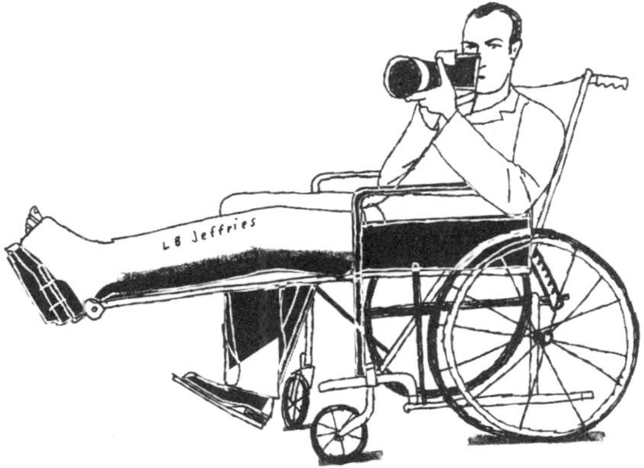

INDEX DES TITRES

GRAPHISTE, ILLUSTRATEUR ET AFFICHISTE,
PAUL ROGERS EST NÉ EN 1957 À LOS ANGELES.
IL VIT À PASADENA, CALIFORNIE.

WWW.PAULROGERSSTUDIO.COM

QUEL est-ce FILM ?
DE PAUL ROGERS
A ÉTÉ ACHEVÉ D'IMPRIMER EN AOÛT 2012
SUR LES PRESSES DE L'IMPRIMERIE TIEN WAH PRESS.

ÉDITIONS CAMBOURAKIS
2, RUE DU MARCHÉ-POPINCOURT
F-75011 PARIS
WWW.CAMBOURAKIS.COM

DÉPÔT LÉGAL : OCTOBRE 2012
ISBN : 978-2-36624-005-4
IMPRIMÉ À SINGAPOUR.

PAUL NEWMAN QUENTIN TARANTINO WARREN JEFF

JOSEPH COTTEN BILLY WILDER BEATTY

STANLEY JACK NICHOLSON SHIRLEY MARTIN BRIDGES

KUBRICK JANET LEIGH JEAN-LUC GODARD MacLAINE SCORSESE JACK LEMMON

PRESTON STURGES AL PACINO

WILLIAM MEL BROOKS JOHN CAZALE GRACE ROMAN

HOLDEN STEVEN SPIELBERG JOHN HOUSTON KELLY POLANSKI